DAWN,

Great

work o[n]

Enjoy the [...]

MESSAGE !

Dr. Rich
Sept 2014
Atlanta

MW00441153

EVERYDAY
LEADER HEROES

EVERYDAY
LEADER HEROES

DR. RICH SCHUTTLER

Everyday Leader Heroes. Copyright © 2013 by Dr. Rich Schuttler.
All rights reserved.
Printed in the United States of America.

No part of this book may be used or reproduced in any manner whatsoever without written permission except in the case of brief quotations embodied in critical articles and reviews. For information, address Caboodle Publishing at P.O. Box 460303, Aurora, CO 80046-0303.

This publication is designed to provide information in regard to the subject matter covered. In so doing, neither the publisher nor the author is engaged in rendering legal, accounting or other professional services. If you require legal advice or other expert assistance, you should seek the services of a professional specializing in the particular discipline required.

While the author has made every effort to provide accurate information at the time of publication, neither the publisher nor the author assumes any responsibility for errors, or for changes that occur after publication.

Caboodle Publishing books may be purchased for educational, business or sales promotional use. For information, please write:
Special Promotions Department, Caboodle Publishing, P.O. Box
460303, Aurora, CO 80046-0303.

FIRST EDITION
Published by Caboodle Publishing, Denver, CO.
Cover design – Caboodle Marketing, Inc.

ISBN: 978-0-9788799-8-3
ISBN-10: 0-9788799-1-0
10 9 8 7 6 5 4 3 2 1

Contents

SECTION 1—The Foundational Understanding For Everyday Leader Heroes

SECTION—Characteristics Of Everyday Leader Heroes

FOREWORD

Dr. Rich Schuttler has done an amazing job of putting together a *must-read* for anyone who is interested in creating success in today's challenging economy. The section on paying tribute to the teachers in your life is a priceless lesson on how to be thankful and become a champion. The stories and co-authors in this book, all from many different backgrounds, will give you brilliant insight on and how you should define success in your life. I found the flow of the book very fluent and the content exceptional.

Success is not only defined by the wealth you have generated but indeed by the quality of the relationships in your life. The outcome you will have when you read *Everyday Leader Heroes* is that you will understand the principles necessary to find balance. You will also realize a number of core characteristics required to find success and happiness in your life. To Dr. Rich, great job of putting together a number of fresh insights to winning in life and what it takes to become tomorrow's hero!

Bill Walsh
Venture Capitalist/Business Coach
Powerteam International
www.pti360.com

This book is dedicated to all those who,
whether knowingly or not, set a great example for
the rest of us to follow;
for you are one of the many everyday leader heroes
of our world!

LEADING LEADERS TO LEAD THEMSELVES SERIES

Leadership Self-Assessment

INTRODUCTION

This book is a result of two years of labor and love as well as 30 years' worth of observations and discussions. The process of writing this book allowed me a special opportunity to reflect on those whom so many others and I admire—everyday leader heroes. The real people in this book's stories are those who selflessly help or have helped others and have thus made a huge difference. Many everyday leader heroes did not purposely set out to be reflected as such; nonetheless, they have made a huge difference in the lives of others.

It was with disappointment that I discovered during the creation of this book that too many everyday leader heroes do not or did not know the impact of their work or words on others. This book is intended to help give notice to those who are doing so much for so many yet do not even realize their own impact.

It is my hope that one of the two situations occurs:

- You have been given this book because you are a leader hero to someone else
- After finishing this book, you'll give it to your leader hero with a nice thank-you note for what they have done for you.

This is a book with stories, real stories from real people about special people—stories that you, the reader, can relate to. If readers can gain insights from these stories, then perhaps they will go out and thank others who have likewise served as inspirational figures to them. This gives credit where credit is due and allows everyday leader heroes to know how they influenced your life, **because they might not know.**

For the past 30 years, I have seen people rise to the top of their professions and stay there while many others rose to the top then ruined their careers, reputations, businesses, and family lives by making poor decisions. No one has ever studied in their executive MBA programs *how to ruin a career or a business*, or *how to hurt others and their own reputation*—but these things happen. Alarmingly, it tends to happen more to those who are highly educated than those who are not.

I have seen many who rose to the top of their professions and failed; examples I did not want to emulate or be like. The process of writing this book about leaders has enabled me to spend a lot of time reflecting on my own actions. Some were noble and some were less than noble. At times I have made bad choices, and while I did learn from them, some experiences unfortunately continue teaching me important lessons I need to relearn.

I have made many mistakes, some of which might lead some readers to perceive me as a hypocrite since I am writing a book about leader heroes. I, like others, am not perfect, as I have hurt others with some of my poor choices. At times, not knowing better or simply failing to choose what's right, I jeopardized my career and reputation. I suspect I am more like everyone I know who has lived a full life having great accomplishments but, like me, regret some things in their lives.

What started out as an exercise in the classes I teach turned into this book. Over two years ago, I began asking the three questions below to students in advanced leadership and other courses I teach, as well as in seminars I have facilitated around the world. I was also fortunate enough to have several colleagues agree to do the same exercise in their own courses and provide me with their responses (Thanks, Lynne!).

1. **Who have you known, or do you know, from your entire life is the one person who stands out amongst all others as being a *leader hero*?** You must personally know or have known each other to appropriately answer this question. In other words, a famous spiritual or political leader or sports star could not be chosen unless you had an actual personal relationship with that person.

2. **Who is (or was) that person to you?** Many answers referred to parents, grandparents, siblings, teachers, coaches, and friends as leader heroes.

3. **What three characteristics of this chosen leader hero make them special?** Many characteristics were common from thousands provided. I captured the many characteristics provided in question number three from each session, and from all the answers I gathered over two years, I identified the most commonly cited ones and discuss them in this book. The 10 most common leadership characteristics are the essence of this book. While this book provides some heartfelt stories, this book also provides the following:

    Self-Assessment Tool: Determine how you are perceived by others in terms of each attribute. You can also ask others to score you and, with their feedback, find out if there are any disparities with your self-assessment aligns. The information gained from knowing your own self-scored quiz and what others believe provides opportunities for self-improvement. The self-assessment tool follows the last chapter of the book.

    Training Tool: The 10 leader hero characteristics can be applied to training programs. They can also be used to identify who has the propensity to do well in efforts to identify young people who have strong potential to become a good or great leader.

A Prescription for Success: By knowing the most common characteristics of leader heroes, you can identify the ones you want to get better at and begin to become a better leader and perhaps, more importantly, a better person. Become better at each of these, and you are on your way to becoming a great leader, too. I have included the Dr. Rich's Prescription for Success at the conclusion of each chapter for you.

I decided, much like in my first book, *Laws of Communication: the Intersection Where Leadership Meet Employee Performance*, that having others contribute to this book would bring diverse views for readers to learn from. I decided since one of the most common 10 characteristics is 'teacher' that I would write that chapter as that is at the core of what I do—I am a teacher.

For the remaining nine leader characteristics, I looked to those whom I believe, amongst everyone else in my life, exemplified each of the characteristics and assigned them a chapter each to talk about their particular strength. These contributing authors are my leader heroes and are those who make a difference every day with so many, as they have for me. Some of them I know well; some I hope to get to know even more.

This book is about those we admire and all too often have failed to thank for their time, wisdom, and guidance. This book is also a reminder that we have what it takes to create change; by being the best we can be and by helping others to achieve their full potential, we can see our actions take flight and create wonderful ripple effects.

Take your time and complete the following self-assessment. Score your perception as it is today and determine what you would want the score to be 1-year from now. Do realize, changing more than 2-points per year may not be possible. After all—it took your entire life to be who are you are right now. Be realistic and learn much about yourself.

CHAPTER TOPICS: A SELF-ASSESSMENT

		Today's Score	1-Year Goal
1	**Supportive** Provides help, information, empathy, and encouragement. Gives time freely to help others. Creates a loving and nurturing environment.		
2	**Listener** Intentional listener. Attends closely for the purpose of understanding. Present to conversations. Focuses on what the other has to say.		
3	**Caring** Assists others when they are troubled. Makes provisions and watches out for others. Shows compassion or concern about life's problems and solutions.		

4	**_Humble_** Not overly proud or arrogant. Modest, courteous, respectful. Does not view oneself as being above or better than others.		
5	**_Integrity_** Adheres to moral and ethical principles. Possesses soundness of moral character and good sense of direction in life, adhering to these in good and bad times. Executes moral convictions. Upholds the truth. Not persuaded solely by money or personal gain.		
6	**_Knowledgeable_** Possesses or exhibits awareness in career, spirituality, mind, body, and other life matters. Insightful. Demonstrates wisdom and passion for ongoing learning. Well-informed and discerning.		
7	**_Motivator_** Creates an atmosphere for others to be self-motivated. Provides incentives and encourages others. Offers guidance free from value judgments. Helpful.		

8	**Mentor** Role model, coach. Shows subject matter expertise. Helps others. Wise and trusted counselor. Influential sponsor or supporter. Extremely positive. Cares about people. Instructs others in a beneficial and informative manner. Patient, understanding.		
9	**Teacher** Inspires learning. Instructor or facilitator of knowledge. Caring. Leaves lifelong impressions. Freely shares experiences with others for their benefit.		
10	**Positive** Great outlook. Optimistic. Encourages others. Confident in one's opinion or assertion. Constructive and fully assured. Not skeptical. Showing or expressing approval or agreement. Favorable, supportive.		
		Total:	

Scoring Considerations

There is no set scientific or calculated points suggesting what is the best or even an ideal score for each *leader hero* attribute or collectively when added together. The results are more so about you gaining new insights about yourself. With that, some of my own *personal* general advice is as follows:

➤ **Low scores (below 4)** in any one attribute or more than one may suggest opportunities for improvement that might be worthy of discussing with another you trust and confide. Low scores overall could suggest maturity growth opportunities and greater social skills would be beneficial. A low score in only one area may offer an insight to how you act or react to others in certain situations. Feedback is helpful from others though power also comes from you thinking about the attributes and planning for a better you.

➤ **Mid-range scores (4-7)** in all areas may offer opportunities for great maturity to become a better family member, friend, or colleague. Only a few scores in the mid-range could be considered as a 'group' where one may influence the other. For example, if one scores low in "Humble" that could relate to a lower score also in "Caring" as people who lack humility are often perceived as not caring.

Discussing your score with another opens the opportunity for them to help you see what you may not be able to see or perceive about yourself.

➤ **High scores (8-10)** may suggest or confirm you are a good or even a great leader. Yet, we all have opportunities for improvement. If you self-score high in all areas, you may still find a discussion with family, friends, and colleagues of value to move yet to a greater extent in the next year. Or, you may have a tendency to over-score yourself. With feedback, fine-tuning is easier when it comes from those who care about you the most. This tool can be reviewed regularly to remind you of what is important and if you make plans to improve in one or more attributes, to remind you of your plan and goals.

Conclusion

It is my intent to offer simple to use tools to help others easily self-assess and self-reflect in regards to personal and professional matters. It has been my experience that those who are able to *look within* and open to feedback are far better friends, colleagues, and citizens then those who do not. You do not need to get better at everything all at once, just find one or two areas that are important and then make incremental gains on a regular basis to achieve your goals and greater success.

SECTION 1

The Foundational Understanding For Everyday Leader Heroes

Chapter 1

What are Everyday Leader Heroes–The Heart of the Matter and a Matter of Fact

By Dr. Rich Schuttler

Everyday Leader Heroes is a title and description born from a repeated realization over the years of lived experiences that caused me to learn and re-learn that the world is desperate for those who will lead. This harsh reality seems to be ever more critical and urgent in such historic times when people who were once trusted have failed, and failed big! Look around at those who have failed and caused damage in our businesses, our schools, our churches, our government, and in our homes. How does something like this happen in a time when there is more information, education, awareness and technology available to leaders than ever before?

In the university programs that my colleagues and I teach, we teach students on how to succeed, not how to fail. Our capstone courses are created to allow students to plan successful profitable organizations, not to run them into the ground. There are no psychology courses that focus on colossal personal failure—failure that hurts co-workers and family members, yet so many leaders do just that. No one sits in their executive MBA program with the intention to ruin their careers, their businesses, or hurt their reputations, yet it happens all too often. And this type of failure needs to stop!

We have all heard of great people who have made positive differences in others' lives and who have set such high standards of what it means to be a hero. Unfortunately, we seem to quickly forget the military heroes who died for our country, or courageous individuals who ran into a burning building to save a family—leader heroes who put their own self-interest after the well-being of others, or who have struggled to champion a cause much bigger than themselves. This book is about these people, those who have gone unnoticed or left unthanked for their selfless efforts. These are the people who "got it right," who have provided and still provide a beacon of hope and inspiration for the rest of us.

The Good

While there is much doom and gloom that populates our 24/7 news shows, there are also many stories about successful leaders that have never been shared. These people are the teachers in elementary schools and high schools who do their very best to teach our world's youth. They are the business leaders who get it right and set a great example for others to emulate, and who went from good to great. They are the sports athletes who realize the value of the positions they have achieved. Whether they realize it or not, they are a beacon of hope for others who admire and aspire to be like them. The good is in our family members, friends, co-workers, and coaches, ordinary people we encounter in our everyday lives.

Cable News Network (CNN) annually honors everyday heroes around the world who are nominated for their exemplary actions. Other organizations award scholarships and prizes to those who set an example that can excite and inspire others to do the same. Award shows and programs honor the world's 'best of the best' in a multitude of venues, whether it is global, national, or local to one's neighborhood. In spite of the many award ceremonies, far too many others rightfully deserve more credit and a big "thank you."

The Real

During the last two years, I have been on a journey with a purpose: to find who our heroes are and how to create more of them. I am blessed to be able to speak with thousands each year around the world in academic classrooms, seminar events, webinars, airplanes, airports, trains, and in more places than I can even recall. I have asked thousands of people whom they admire the most as far as leaders they look up to, and why they do so.

I was expecting to hear names of famous people from government, entertainment, sports, religious, and other sectors, where we most commonly hear of well-known leadership figures.

To my surprise, that was not what I heard. Over and over, I heard about selfless individuals who sacrificed for other members of their family. I heard about high school janitors who tutored high school students in math after school. I heard about teachers people had in their youth that, today, after 20 or more years, leave memories and lessons that are likely to be remembered for a lifetime. I heard about everyday people who, while in part might have been obligated or expected to set an example, did far more than that and went beyond the call of duty.

My path has led me to start wondering about and capturing what I have learned. Doing so has caused me to think deeply and even cry at the beauty and simplistic reality of who the real heroes are in our world. The unfortunate finding in all this was that, in most cases these people of quality rarely ever knew they were and are considered by others to be everyday leader heroes. That certainly was the case for me and my heroes; I recall rarely ever telling them, at the time or even since then. This also has to change; these people need to know the huge difference they made or are making in the lives of others before it is too late.

These realizations also caused me to look inward to determine who I thought were great leaders. In a quiet time and space, I thought about the people whom I believed were the heroes who set a great example for me and made a difference in who I am today. For me, they are a high school teacher (Mr. John Watts) who gave me more than an education, a military officer (Lieutenant Commander Tim Reynolds) who gave me my first opportunity to lead a team, an uncle (Stephen Miske) who had polio but refused to allow that to stop him from living a full life, and my mother (Irene Miske-Kornecki) who, when my father died when I was 10 years old and my sister was 15 years old, made sure that her children were taken care of and had as many opportunities as any other child in the world.

The Why

I have long wanted to identify common characteristics of successful people who have been referred to as heroes by so many others. I wanted to do this as I noticed far too many so-called leaders who fell from grace, ruining their careers and hurting their families, and yet were admired by many prior to their downfall. I wanted to find ways to stop such cycles of loss of credibility. I wanted to then take my findings to help create programs to better educate and train young people who want to become great leaders—or, at least, better identify those who have shown leadership potential at an early age.

This book is about those who took and continue to take action. This chapter offers insights into common views that many leader heroes hold. It is about everyday heroes, as described by so many for more than a two-year period, those who have some characteristics that may suggest why they are so proudly spoken of by so many. The "difference makers" are easily remembered but are all too often taken for granted despite their contributions. This book will help such underappreciated individuals to receive the credit long due to them.

Leadership Is a Contact Sport

A friend and colleague (Dr. John Latham) remarked that "leadership is a contact sport." Yet in every sport, there are more than just the players on the field. There are the coaches, the owners, the vendors, and the audiences, each of whom may either be active or not but make the games possible.

Those leaders who have left an indelible spirit on others have also made their mistakes and have their regrets. What makes everyday leader heroes great is their ability to move forward, doing the best they can and not being afraid to look in the mirror while taking inventory of who is in the reflection. These heroes developed into great leaders and then helped others; they took action!

Everyday leader heroes are often noted for their uncanny ability to recognize, but more so to communicate that there is always a way to improve any given situation. This perspective can be provided in a one-on-one relationship from someone we look up to and from whom we seek advice—take, for example an organization leader that provides confidence to employees.

Leading means "stepping up to the plate" or getting involved when needed without having to be asked to get involved. It may be the person walking down the street who finds a piece of litter and picks it up and puts it in a trash receptacle, or someone who, when there is work to be done takes action and gets the job done willfully and by his own initiative. One does not have to have a formal title to take action in order to lead. In most instances, our everyday leader heroes are just doing the work that needs to be done in a manner that subsequently brings great credit upon them.

Pioneers and Settlers

In early times, in undiscovered countries, those few who went out first into the wilderness before others did so to explore new territories. They did this to gain information and knowledge that was not yet known. These explorers were often referred to as pioneers. These pioneers took risks, often putting their lives on the line, to explore what was not known so that they could return with the experiences of their journey to share with others who were to follow later. These risks were taken to ensure it would be safer for others to follow and to expand into uncharted territories.

Today's leader heroes, much like in the past are known for going forward first and at times risking everything so that they can follow their own intuition or dreams in search for what is not known. Leader heroes are much like the characters in the science fiction series *Star Trek*, who state that their mission is "to boldly go where no one has gone before©." Leader heroes are modern day explorers charting unknown territories.

Settlers are those who take the information from the pioneers' exploration and later follow to establish a new community and to allow many more who want to follow to do so safely. Settlers, unlike pioneers, establish the norms for those who will later become part of a new community. Settlers are important, as they bring order to a new beginning. With their focus on improving processes and procedures, they help leader heroes pave the way for motivated followers unified with a common vision.

Leader heroes are found in both entrepreneurial pioneers as well as in intrapreneurial settlers. Oftentimes, leader heroes intentionally set out to make a difference. Others do not but, through their solid work habits, do so anyway.

Thermostat or Thermometer

A thermostat sets the temperature whereas a thermometer merely reflects the temperature. Leader heroes are like thermostats setting an appropriate climate conducive to success. These thermostats, or leader heroes, are responsible for setting the vision of an organization. The climate they set includes trust and respect for others, as they know that without either, communication will break down and the climate will be uncomfortable for everyone. Whether in times of calm or of high stress, leader heroes seek better ways to show others that their best days are yet to come.

As a thermostat does, a leader hero who perceives that the climate is no longer comfortable for everyone will take action and adjust the temperature as needed to ensure comfort for everyone involved. Knowing when to change the climate setting is critical because leader heroes can sense when such changes are needed and can then take the necessary actions to make it happen.

Other leaders like a thermometer, reflect and understand the climate and are entrusted to follow through, maintain, and achieve the highest levels of efficiency and effectiveness to accomplish the vision of the organization as set by the thermostat or leader hero. These leaders develop the mission steps necessary to maintain the climate using their followers and processes. Although these leaders are not responsible for changing the climate, they can and often affect whether or not the current climate is the one needed for the good of the organization. They work within the level of the organization wherein communication problems commonly occur, so they best know when to inform the leader hero that a climate change is necessary.

True leader heroes move beyond maintaining the status quo and are always looking to move well away from a kind of "box thinking" that hampers creativity and innovation. The "thermostat" leaders will be the entrepreneurs who are first to the marketplace with a new product or service, one that soon becomes a cultural norm. Steve Jobs, with his vision for Apple products, was one such example of a thermostat leader.

Kleenex™ is an example of a cultural norm. Although many others similar products now exist, most people still refer to the soft tissues as Kleenex regardless of the brand. John Kimberly was president of Kimberly Clark in 1924 when the brand name "Kleenex" was coined. Kimberly is a leader hero because of his visionary marketing strategies, which established the cultural icon now known as Kleenex. Steve Jobs and John Kimberly are examples of visionaries able to conceive new ideas and ways to do things differently to get better results.

Looking to solve the complex problems of tomorrow, leader heroes purposely look to the future and set out to create a new or better product or service to eliminate problems before they become a reality. Some leader heroes are also known as futurists, who, with their intuition, can foresee the needs of people before the people themselves even know it. Futurists are systematic thinkers who look to make the future a better place through the development of breakthrough strategies.

Self-Reflect, Self-Assess, and Self-Correct

Leader heroes as previously noted are rarely perfect people. In fact, they are flawed, just as most people are. At one time or another they have made mistakes. The difference is that these heroes then found a way to overcome their mistakes. They did not get involved in a self-created *pity party*; instead they learned from their experiences and exhibited their ability to climb above their mistakes. More importantly, they found ways to share their learning with others in hopes of keeping others from making the same mistakes.

Self-Reflect

The ability to self-reflect may be one of the most important skills a person can learn. Reflecting on what has already happened can provide insights to make the present as well as the future better than it would be otherwise. Reflecting on past personal experiences, realizing what happened, and then determining the positive outcomes as well as the opportunities for improvement allows for learning to occur. Self-reflection facilitates the learning process.

The U.S. Army and many other organizations apply an *After Action Review* as a method to analyze a prior battle or exercise in an effort to learn from it and to help ensure that the next time something similar happens, a better result occurs. People do the same thing when they reflect upon past situations and certain periods in their lives. For some, reflecting is done in a diary or a journal; for others it is a discussion that takes place with two or more people related to the experience.

Self-Assess

From self-reflection, one can then self-assess their actions and the outcomes. For those of us who have been in trouble from time to time for making poor choices, self-reflection allows for replaying the situation that occurred and allows for self-assessment. Looking at the way we acted or reacted and understanding why we did what we did can be helpful in preventing similar situations from recurring.

One should replay what occurred and determine their situation in what transpired. Much like watching a movie of the experience, one can stop or move slowly through the experience, analyzing why decisions were made and how the decisions affected the outcome. From this self-assessment, one can determine what they would do if such a situation were to arise again.

Whether it is a worker who accidentally violated a safety policy or military exercises, or words haphazardly spoken that could not be taken back, the ability to self-assess, like any other skill, needs to be practiced in order to be refined. Leader heroes are skilled at assessing their actions and their words; they need this quality to continually self-improve as a leader and, more importantly, as a person.

Self-Correct

While the skills to self-assessment and self-reflection are both important, they mean little if one does not or cannot self-correct. The difference between learning from a mistake and knowing why it happened differs from disallowing the same situation from happening again in the future. Self-correcting means learning from a past situation and then purposely taking steps to ensure it does not happen again. Many people with addictive behaviors know they should not repeat their harmful behaviors yet are unfortunately unable to self-correct, thus allowing the downward cycle to repeat itself.

Self-correcting is what many leader heroes are able to do effortlessly, as it is an innate or refined skill to them. They not only learn from their mistakes, but they also learn from watching others who have made such mistakes. More importantly, they refrain from repeating the same blunders. Leader heroes are able to focus on being a better person and helping others to learn from their own errors. Many of the heroes you will read about have made mistakes but were able to rise above and turn things around.

Example

Self-reflecting, self-assessing, and self-correcting are skills that need to be practiced and refined over time. Journaling and being in an environment that provides for great association with others are ways to hone and perfect these kills. Self-correcting is then what leaders do; they take action on what they have learned and know how to do better in the future.

Self-reflecting is more than just looking back at a situation and thinking that one should not have done whatever they did. For example, if one touches a hot stove, one can reflect back on the burning of their hand, but that does little by itself to preclude it from happening again. One needs to look into how and why something happened as well as the surrounding environment to gain a better understanding of the entire situation that led to the event. This is illustrated in the Learning Lifecycle, Figure 1.1 below.

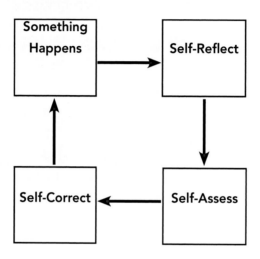

Leader heroes are those who are continually striving to become better. Leader heroes are those in our lives who help us to become a better person as well, whether they are aware of what they are doing or not. In most instances, those we look up to as leader heroes have no real understanding of what they are doing to have such a significant impact, yet they continue to do it in a manner that suggests everyone is in the midst of greatness.

Perspective

Leader heroes tend to have a common attribute of letting what does not truly matter slide. In essence, they are able to prioritize and make decisions based on what is important—whether that be personally or professionally. Many successful leaders will prioritize their work with lists that they update regularly to reflect where they should focus their time and energy to achieve the greatest impact. Leader heroes have life skills that go beyond keeping lists to maintain priorities, however. They have an inherent ability to live life on their own terms, thus paving way for a life that is focused and purposeful.

Letting the small things slide is found in work or other priorities that compete for leader heroes' time and thoughts. Leader heroes appear to have a view of the future but are also realistic in what today's challenges mean to them as well as those around them. After communicating with a leader hero, most depart with a sense of ease and confidence that came from the interaction, that somehow, unbeknownst to the leader hero, made everything okay.

When I talk with leader heroes, they seem to have been grounded in what really matters not just to them but also to me. They are able to help me stop evaluating myself by the circumstances of the moment but more so help me to see the fullness of my potential. They offer inspiration for me to have faith and to know that it is possible to achieve my goals and to fulfill my vision. Leader heroes somehow seem to know how to help others go make great things happen.

Opportunities, Not Problems

Leader heroes also have a common view of how they see what is in front of them as compared to how others see the same things. Leader heroes solve the obvious problems others seem to ignore yet do so in a manner by seeing those obvious problems as unique opportunities. Leader heroes look at what has happened and then change the future by doing something different at that moment.

One's context of a given situation dictates their approach. If one sees problems all the time, they tend to be in the "fixing" or "correcting" frame of mind. Problems are often the fault of a system or of people. This *blame game* tends to be a common approach when looking at who is responsible for overcoming problems. Problems need to be corrected for efficiency and effectiveness, but oftentimes they are "fixed," only to return later—much like a fire that has been put out but reignites later.

Leader heroes learn from the past but don't relive it. When leader heroes view a past situation as an opportunity, they tend to see exactly how to improve upon the situation or to arrive at a more pleasant outcome. Leader heroes not only see the opportunity; they also identify and remove the root cause instead of merely eliminating a symptom of the problem. Seeing the chance for improvement is a forward-looking opportunity; problem solving focuses on the present alone.

Convictions

Leader heroes do not have strong convictions about weak issues or weak convictions about significant issues. They have clear, strong convictions that reflect the level of commitment that each matter deserves. These convictions are demonstrated in how leader heroes work and in how they communicate to inspire and motivate others.

Leader heroes do not think you will be a success; they know you will be a success. They communicate this in a manner that allows you to believe it as well. These heroes are not caught up in trivial issues or discussions that don't matter. They engage in dynamic discussions that bring out the best in all those involved, even if it is just one other person. They use an active voice and help those around them to know what goals will be accomplished.

Sure, these leader heroes have opinions, some rather strong, but they can support their opinions with their experiences, education, and insights. You always know where these leaders stand on issues because they tell you and hold true to their convictions. They not only talk about them but also display them. As the saying goes, they "walk the talk."

These leaders, while reflecting their own convictions, also do not try to make you believe the same things they do. They are better than that! They'll help others to see through the surface of things, to notice suitable alternatives, to ask hard questions and to develop their own convictions. What is most important from such exchanges with these leader heroes is that they move others to find their passions and convictions, and they model behavior that allows for the sharing of thoughts without offensiveness or arrogance.

Self-Views

Many leader heroes hold high-level career positions, yet more often than not, our heroes are family members, neighbors, teachers, and coaches. Two common characteristics of leader heroes are the fact that they usually are not impressed by their successes, nor are they intimidated by their failures.

Leader heroes are comfortable with their past and are proud of how they have matured. Some are young people while many are older, possessing a robust richness of lessons learned and achievements that they do not brag about.

Leader heroes remember the lessons they learned from the "school of hard knocks." They remain humble in their views of themselves and of those around them. Leader heroes go out of their way to help others achieve greater success even when they themselves have already attained it. These leader heroes, while not compelled to do so, often have a sense of "giving back" to the less privileged, or to those who need a break or who simply need a little support and inspiration.

Turning Nothing into Something

Everyday leader heroes seem to have an inherent ability to not only turn a problem into an opportunity but can also turn nothing into something. After all, these unique people are not only dreamers; they are also doers— living and fulfilling their dreams. These people of action not only believe in their own dreams but also in the dreams of others.

These leaders have a vision much like John F. Kennedy when he stated his vision of putting a man on the moon before the end of the 1960s. His vision provided the means for the mission to begin the actual work to achieve that feat by the end of that decade. Leader heroes turn nothing into something by creating a vision, communicating it, and getting others excited and involved in making it happen. This is how leader heroes create history.

Practicing the art of the impossible seems effortless for the leaders we admire. They are the pioneers, those who set the culture and create the path for the rest to follow. These leader heroes are true optimists and see the best in everything. The proverbial glass is neither viewed as half empty nor half full but is always overflowing abundantly.

Leader heroes not only think outside the box; they also let go of the box completely and often start anew. They have mastered the skill of forgetting what is behind, instead march towards what lies ahead. They see the better way and encourage others to glimpse forward as well. Our leader heroes are focused people always looking for a better way; they concentrate a little longer and a little harder. They not only make commitments but they also live up to them as well.

Leader heroes learn from the past but do not live in the past. They realize life's biggest challenges will bring difficulties, but they do not dwell on them. They learn from them. In order to let go of the box, learn from the past, constantly strive to move forward and find better ways, they concentrate on what lies ahead without dwelling on potential difficulties that might await. Leader heroes must choose their friends carefully so that all this can happen as smoothly as possible.

Perseverance

Leader heroes are willing to accept what comes their way knowing that no matter what happens they will win and come out stronger. They have the determination to stand firm while others fail or fall away.

Our leader heroes are not only able to do these things themselves but can also mentor and guide others in similar ways.

This is much like the athlete who realizes it is more challenging to stay healthy and productive in professional sports than the challenges in rising to the top to become a professional athlete. An athlete's speed and intensity to become a professional is more important than the challenges faced on the path to get there. The everyday leader heroes we admire realize that it is much like the fictional character Rocky Balboa said to his son, "It's not how hard life hits, it's how hard we can get hit and still get up to keep going."

Insight to See Character Develop

Of all the characteristics you will read about in this book, perhaps the most common of all the others is that everyday leader heroes have a unique insight to see and help develop character in others. Perhaps since they have been through a number of life's challenges and have learned from the "school of hard-knocks," they have self-reflected, self-assessed, and self-corrected a number of times, learning more and more lessons from each cycle.

Life's lessons produce people who realize that how they view the world and live their lives reflects opportunities. Along with the ability to see what others cannot see and the perseverance to keep going when one's dream or vision seems impossible to achieved, they have developed their own character and have the knowledge and skill to show others how they can do the same.

The leader heroes I have known each have the ability to help me find the unrealized potential I have within me. Whether it is in an encouraging word, a given opportunity, or a discussion that provides me with new information to ponder, the help and guidance I have received from these leaders allowed me to let go of blinders and move beyond self-imposed boundaries. They encouraged me to seek what I thought was unearned responsibility and accountability. They taught me to view myself not for who I was but rather for the potential of who I could become.

Beginning at the End

This book is written to help you understand that we go through our lives too often unappreciative of the leader heroes we have encountered, those people who have helped shape who we are and what we do. It is my hope that you will stop and identify who those people were and are in your life that are everyday leader heroes, then find a way to let them and their families know the profound effect they have had on your life. Then, emulate them to the best of your ability—that will in turn bring even greater credit upon them!

In my years of travel and teaching, I have identified the characteristics I believe must be present in every leader hero. But they are not those that I only hold to be true but of thousands of people around the world in different industries and of different ages. These characteristics are provided in this book for you to have and to share with others who can also benefit from knowing them.

I ask that you look at these characteristics retrospectively and see which ones lie within you and identify you as a leader hero. Ask yourself these questions and think about each before answering:

- Who have I tried to inspire, motivate, or simply provide a gentle positive suggestion to in the past?
- What are my dreams for myself and for others around me? What am I doing to accomplish them?
- Do I look at my life as being half empty, half full, or overflowing with excitement and dreams for the future?
- Who have I taught something important to?
- Have I mentored someone and looked at their success with a sense of self-satisfaction and great accomplishment?

- Do I feel comfortable not just communicating my thoughts, feelings, and ideas to others, but do I also listen to their thoughts, feelings and ideas?

After reflecting on these questions, I suggest you consider each of the stories in this book. I trust that you will find the leader hero qualities that you already possess or that you can develop even further. If you make a mistake, admit it right away and seek help in correcting it and making things better for all concerned. Then you will have applied the characteristic of a real everyday leader hero and will be able to answer the question, "Am I an everyday leader hero?" with a resounding, "Yes!"

Dr. Rich's Prescription for Success

Mirror, Mirror on the Wall: A Five-Minute Self-Reflection Exercise

1. Go into a quiet room by yourself and stand roughly three feet in front of a mirror. A bedroom or bathroom will do just fine for this exercise.

2. The mirror should be at least large enough for you to see your entire face.

3. Turn off your music, television, and cell phone, and eliminate all background noise as well as any potential distractions. If you have pets, put them outside or in another room during this exercise so that they do not disturb or distract you.

4. Stand in front of the mirror and look into your own eyes.

5. Focus on looking into your eyes, but not in the typical "grooming areas" such as where you normally look for your make-up or wrinkles.

6. For five minutes focus on looking into your own eyes.

7. The first 60 to 90 seconds may be uncomfortable. If you sense your eyes are losing focus, reframe and

concentrate again on intentionally looking into your own eyes.

8. After 90 seconds, most people start to get more comfortable. As one becomes more interested in the person they see in the reflection, they are less easily distracted.

9. Let your thoughts go where they may, but remain looking into your own eyes.

10. You can stop after about 5 minutes.

This is simple for many yet difficult for others. For some it is a challenging exercise that can be enlightening. For others it can seem to be a waste of time. For those who find this enlightening, common results tend to be a greater sense of awareness of who you are, in a manner that reflects on the past and offers a glimpse of present day self-evaluation. For those who sense no outcome from the exercise, this might suggest you were not able to focus enough, or perhaps it will take more than one attempt to gain insights about yourself that you have yet to realize.

Some find it helpful to journal about their experience and to use this journal as a learning diary that captures all of the important reflections they continue to gain through self-assessment in their maturing process.

Moving Through the 10 Most Common Leadership Characteristics of Real People

As you read through the 10 most common characteristics of everyday real people, you will likely remember family members, friends, colleagues and those who are or have been near and dear to you. This is because the characteristics or lessons will remind you of special people who have been part of your life. As you go through the characteristics, write down the names of those who come to mind.

When done, take your list of names and start thanking them for all they have done for you. Let them know the impact they had or are having on your life. A card or letter of appreciation always makes one feel better. The art of being a leader hero means having the skills to communicate with others in different ways that are reflective of kindness and appreciation. If you can't find some of the people or if they have passed on, find another way to give credit where credit is due and show appreciation for the value they have provided.

Chapter 1: Everyday Leader Heroes

Dr. Rich Schuttler is a customer-driven & quality-focused innovative and engaging international public speaker, educator, and author. He possesses 25 years' worth of diversified, domestic, and international management and leadership improvement expertise within academic, federal/state governments, and *Fortune 1000* environments developing strategies and implementation methods. Rich has mentored executives, faculty, and students from around the world in a variety of professional leadership and management settings. He served in the U.S. Navy and retired after 23 years of honorable service in the field of cryptology. Dr. Rich is the author of *Laws of Communication: The Intersection Where Leadership Meets Employee Performance. He a co-founder of Professional Progress Academy and online educational and training membership site (www. proprogressacademy.com)*.

CHAPTER 2

Success by Design:
Scholar–Practitioner–Leader

Contributed By Dr. Dennis R. Clodi

Leadership Research

For years, researchers debated whether leaders were born or made. Equally long debates centered on whether or not success as a leader can be predicted are still taking place. Why are some people successful as leaders while others are not? I see people in every field or profession who are successful and some who are not. What is it that those who succeed have or do that those who fail do not? Is it education, money, social networks, lottery winnings, inheritance, hard work, honesty or a positive attitude? All of these could be a part of the answer, but none of them stand alone.

Traits vs. Characteristics

Researchers differentiate between traits and characteristics. Traits have to do with the quality of a person's behavior that reflects their personality. People are born with certain traits. A person has a particular set of traits that causes them to behave in similar ways regardless of the situation in which they find themselves.

Characteristics are attributes that are developed or acquired throughout a person's life starting with birth. Babies are not born criminals, but some turn out to be. The values of those who raise them and the environment in which they are raised are what lead some children to grow up to commit vile crimes. A case can be made that certain learned characteristics contribute to people reaching various degrees of success or failure.

Traits are inherent while characteristics are developed. I think understanding the difference between the two is important because researchers have been trying to understand how to predict a person's success as a leader. Since characteristics are acquired, those can be more easily identified than traits and are more likely to be indicators of leadership success.

Ten Characteristics for Leadership Success

In this book, we talk about the 10 characteristics related to being a successful leader. These characteristics were identified through research conducted by Dr. Rich Schuttler. During years of consulting work, he asked people in groups, workshops and one-on-one conversations three questions:

1. Who, of everyone you have known in your entire life, is the one person who stands out amongst all others as being a leader hero? The person identified had to be someone the interviewee knew and vice versa. Those answering could not choose a famous spiritual or political leader or sports star unless an actual personal relationship between the two people existed.

2. Who is (or was) that person to you? People answering this question cited parents, grandparents, siblings, teachers, coaches, and friends as their leader heroes.

3. What three characteristics do (or did) you identify with the chosen leader hero? Thousands of characteristics were provided as answers to this question.

Dr. Schuttler took the thousands of answers he received and reduced them to the 10 most common characteristics of leader heroes. He felt that a person who was aware of these common characteristics of leader heroes could use them as a way to become a better person and a better leader.

The Scholar-Practitioner-Leader Model

The University of Phoenix, School of Advanced Studies, has a leadership model that is a thread throughout their doctoral program. The Scholar-Practitioner-Leader (SPL) is closely related to the characteristics discussed in this book. It also sheds light on the experiences of the people I have used as examples in this chapter. I want to relate the 10 characteristics to the three parts of the SPL model.

Scholar	Knowledgeable	Has expertise in his or her field or profession
	Mentor	Shows subject matter expertise and willingness to coach and instruct others
	Teacher	Inspires learning or is a facilitator of knowledge
Practitioner	Supportive	Provides help and information
	Listener	Present in conversations, focuses on what others are communicating
	Motivator	Encourages others, provides guidance free from value judgments, provides incentives
	Mentor	Is positive, patient, understanding; a role model and a coach
	Teacher	Inspires learning, shares freely with others

	Caring	Shows compassion or concern for others, assists others when they are troubled
	Humble	Is respectful and courteous and not arrogant
Leader	Positive	Shows optimism and a great outlook; encourages others and is confident in his or her opinions
	Humble	Is respectful and courteous and not arrogant
	Integrity	Adheres to moral and ethical practices; has a good sense of direction in life and remains steadfast in good and bad times; is not persuaded solely by money or personal gain
	Motivator	Encourages others, provides guidance free from value judgments, provides incentives
	Teacher	Inspires learning and shares freely with others

Being Smart Is Not Enough

I have three degrees and five state certificates. I have State Board Association training in collective bargaining negotiations. I am a trainer of trainers for teachers, parents and administrators operating federally funded substance abuse programs. I wrote a book for parents and teachers on substance abuse. I have written articles about the state of education in the nation. I wrote and received millions of dollars in state and federal grants used to train over 8,000 teachers in Illinois on how to design lessons where students were responsible for their own work. I have written training workbooks used in different kinds of training seminars. In short, I have plenty of education.

Misery Loves Company

In spite of all my education, in my first three years as a school principal I was a failure as a leader. I had all the knowledge I needed. I held all of the degrees and certificates my position required. I cared very much about having my staff develop classes that helped students learn better. Why did I fail? I was not a good listener. I was the boss and I told people what to do. I was not supportive of my staff because I arrogantly felt I knew more than they did. I was anything but humble. After all, I was a *doctor*. I tried, but failed, to motivate the staff. I certainly wasn't able to teach them anything.

None of the staff wanted me to be their mentor. I believed I had integrity. However, without the persuasion of money or personal gain, I really didn't have much integrity either. I wanted to build a career that would get me a job in a large school district as a superintendent or as a company CEO where I could make a lot of money. Although I thought I had a positive attitude, the staff perceived me as being very negative towards them. They refused to follow me at all. They told me within my first three months on the job, "We were here when you came and we'll be here when you leave." They were right. I was missing eight of the 10 characteristics that a successful leader has. I was miserable, and so was my staff.

What About the Scholar-Practitioner-Leader?

During the time I was a school principal, I had the scholar part of the SPL model. I had been through all the learning expected of scholars. Even though I had the title of principal, I could not function as a leader because I lacked the practice—the practice of applying all that I had learned. I acted reactively rather than proactively. I was always reacting to the pushback I got from my staff; I could not "practice" my scholarly knowledge, and thus never went through the necessary steps for becoming an effective leader.

As a scholar, I was knowledgeable of the characteristics needed to be a successful leader, but because of my lack of skills as a practitioner, I failed as a leader. Having only 8 of the 10 leader hero characteristics and only two parts of the SPL model, it certainly did not make me an effective leader.

What a Difference a Mentor Makes

Eventually, I moved into a new district where I was an assistant superintendent. My boss was an outstanding mentor. He took me under his wing and guided me as I worked to become a good administrator and leader. I still made mistakes, but he was always there to teach me what I had done wrong and how I could have handled things differently. He always maintained a positive attitude with me when I made a mistake. He was infinitely patient and compassionate. When I didn't know how to approach a particular situation, he was there to listen, support and teach me. Because he cared about me, he taught me how to care about others staff and how to listen to staff members.

Success Is...

My mentor's district achieved great success. The district, through his leadership, received many state and national awards, yet he never took any credit for those successes. It was always his staff that accomplished great things. This man remained humble throughout everything the district achieved.

"If it ain't broken, break it!'" was a commonly heard motto in my mentor's district. He always wanted his staff to look critically at what they were doing to see if improvements were possible. Looking back at his personal and professional life, I see in him the characteristics that spell success: teacher, listener, a motivator and a mentor; caring and compassionate, ethical, knowledgeable and positive.

In the case of my mentor, he exhibited all parts of the SPL model. He had the degrees needed to be a scholar. He was an award-winning teacher and a successful principal. He practiced his craft successfully over many years. As a teacher and a principal, he was keenly aware of the characteristics that produced success. That's how he got to be a superintendent in a very large, prestigious school district. He lived the characteristics for success and the SPL model on a daily basis. All these made proved that he was a great leader.

Book Learning Is Not Always the Key

My father is an example of a successful leader despite the fact that he only finished two years of high school. He dropped out of school to get a job to help support his parents and brother. He worked hard and became a master carpenter. He was so successful as a carpenter that he was hired to be a construction superintendent in charge of overseeing the construction of huge projects such as hospitals, schools, and shopping malls. The architects who designed those buildings were so impressed with his self-taught skills that they hired him to be their field architect, the person responsible for ensuring that contractors were following architectural plans. Eventually the firm even had him doing his own building designs.

Why was my father successful? He had no formal education, but being a hard worker and caring about the quality of his work (and of others') partially answer for his success. He was able to motivate others to care about the quality of their work. He was respected because contractors knew he was knowledgeable. He was supportive, caring, knowledgeable, a motivator, a good listener and a mentor to many tradesmen.

Examining my father's success as a leader through the lens of the SPL model, he had accomplished the "scholar" part of the SPL in a completely different way than my mentor and I had. He learned on the job. He learned from others and taught himself the rest of what he needed to know. On the job, learning provided the "practice" part of the model. He practiced many years before he was given a leadership opportunity. My father had no conscious knowledge of the 10 characteristics of successful leaders or the three parts of the SPL model, but because of his value system, how he lived his life, and how he learned and practiced his craft, he gained the characteristics necessary to become a successful leader.

What Does This All Mean?

The three examples I presented show that having some of the 10 characteristics is not sufficient. Moreover, many people might think they possess many or all of the 10 characteristics even though others may not think similarly. If a person possesses all 10 characteristics of leadership but everyone around the person perceives them to have very few or none of them, he or she still can't be a successful leader. Self-assessment may convince you that you should be successful based on the 10 characteristics discussed in this book, but the assessment of those with whom you purport to lead must see you demonstrating those characteristics.

Education is something people acquire, but a formal education is not necessarily required. I know people who have multiple degrees yet are not successful. I know people with little education who are very successful. Education, by itself, does not appear to be the answer to whether or not someone is successful. Having only one part, the scholar part of the SPL model will not by itself ensure that you will be a successful leader. Without it though, you achieving success may prove more challenging.

What Causes Failure?

Is there a minimum number of the 10 characteristics you must possess to be a successful leader? Is there some combination of the 10 characteristics you must possess to be a successful leader? Is there a single attribute that, if lacking, will cause you to fail as a leader? Is there a combination of them that will?

People who are not positive about their work or their colleagues are almost certain to fail. Negative people are rarely supportive of those with whom they work. If you are a negative person, you are not likely to care about the people you work with; you likely won't help them when troubles arise. Negative people do not care about the work to help colleagues in need. Negative people do not care about the personal or work problems of their followers. If a team member is having problems, bosses who are negative and do not care will not provide them with the necessary support. If they do not care about their followers, they will not mentor or teach any of them. Bosses like this will not motivate followers because they just expect them to do their job in return for their salary.

People who don't care about others show little or no respect for others. They will not be courteous. They will lack humility. They will not listen to what others have to say because they know better. Because they don't listen, they won't be flexible. They feel they don't need the input of their followers. They may or may not be knowledgeable, but they will not be perceived as being knowledgeable. Such kinds of "leaders" will have team members who resent how they are treated and will only do the bare minimum required to survive in their positions. They will be working behind the scenes to undermine this kind of leader while they are looking for a better job. Although a person lacking all of the characteristics listed may not be doing anything illegal, they certainly lack a moral integrity relative to how they treat their followers.

What Is Flexibility?

With the rapid changes in technology and consumer demands for better products and services, world-class leaders such as Warren Buffet, Bill Gates, Michael Dell, T. Boone Pickens and Donald Trump recognize the need for successful leaders to be flexible. Trump recently said that when things change and new challenges appear, successful leaders must be flexible enough to go over them, around them, or through them. I have seen highly educated yet inflexible people and they seem to always be struggling to survive. Indeed, flexibility appears to be an important attribute in achieving success as a leader.

The 10 characteristics discussed in this book, based on years of research, do not include flexibility. If I look at the characteristics for each of the 10 characteristics, I can see where flexibility is a combination of being supportive, being a good listener, being caring, having integrity, maintaining a positive attitude, and being a teacher. The successful leaders I use as examples in this chapter had all of the characteristics and are flexible. As I look at the excellent leaders I listed above, all are people who are successful leaders because of their flexibility.

What Happens Next?

After I realized that having advanced degrees was insufficient for me to be a successful leader, I talked with many people I respected as leaders. I studied what successful leaders did that I had not done. I read books that successful leaders had written. I took several leadership assessment surveys. What I discovered was that successful leadership seems to come back to the parts of the scholar-practitioner-leadership model and the 10 characteristics I have discussed throughout the course of this chapter.

I decided there were 20 questions I needed to answer based on the SPL model and the 10 characteristics. I have put the questions into a survey tool you can use to do what I did to see where you need to improve."

- Dr. Dennis Clodi

Dr. Rich's Prescription for Success

1.   Being Smart is not enough—know the other ingredients that you need for a successful recipe.

2.   Misery loves company—so don't invite miserable people to your life's party.

3.   If it ain't broken, break it—take a closer and more focused look at everything you are doing.

4.   Be flexible—think of yourself as a willow in the wind. The branches don't break when a wind storm hits, they bow, bend and are flexible to withstand the storm.

What You Can Ask Yourself?

Circle the number that you feel best describes you. After you answer all 20 questions, add up the total number of points and check the descriptors for your score at the end of the survey tool.

ATTRIBUTES ASSESSMENT TOOL	NOT AT ALL	USUALLY	VERY MUCH SO
CIRCLE ONLY 1 NUMBER IN EACH ROW			

Are you a good LISTENER?	*1*	*2*	*3*
Do others consider you a good LISTENER?	*1*	*2*	*3*
Are you willing to ACCEPT IDEAS from others?	*1*	*2*	*3*
Do you treat others with RESPECT?	*1*	*2*	*3*
Are you an ETHICAL Person?	*1*	*2*	*3*
Do you MOTIVATE others?	*1*	*2*	*3*
Are you an OPTIMISTIC person?	*1*	*2*	*3*
Do you think FOLLOWERS think you are an OPTIMISTIC person?	*1*	*2*	*3*
Are you willing to share YOUR SUCCESSES with others?	*1*	*2*	*3*
Are you KNOWLEDGEABLE?	*1*	*2*	*3*
Do OTHERS believe you are KNOWLEDGEABLE?	*1*	*2*	*3*
Do you consciously try to INSPIRE others?	*1*	*2*	*3*

	1	2	3
Do you care about the PERSONAL problems of your FOLLOWERS?	*1*	*2*	*3*
Do you care about the PROFESSIONAL problems of your FOLLOWERS?	*1*	2	3
Are you a COURTEOUS person?	*1*	2	3
Are you a HUMBLE person?	*1*	2	3
Do others feel you are a HUMBLE person?	*1*	2	3
Are you SUPPORTIVE of ideas of others?	*1*	2	3
Do you MENTOR others?	*1*	2	3
	1	*2*	*3*
TOTAL SCORE			

LOW SCORES (11-29) If your score fell within this range, this may suggest opportunities for improvement that are worthy of self-reflection and discussion with a trusted colleagues. A score in this range may represent insights into your behavior(s) and how others see in you in various situations. Look for ways you can look at the individual scores lower than 3 on each of the questions and work out strategies that could help you improve in those areas.

MID-RANGE SCORES (30-44) If your score fell within this range, this may provide insight for you to become a better leader in both your personal and professional life. You already have several areas where you have self-assessed yourself as a good leader. You need to look at the individual scores lower than 3 and find ways to improve how your see yourself or how others see you.

HIGH SCORES (45-60) Scores in this range represent you are already a good leader in your own eyes and in the eyes of others. Since no person is perfect, discussions about each item with family members or trusted colleagues might provide insight to move from being a good leader to being a great leader. Feedback from others usually provides valuable information on how a person can better himself or herself.

Using this simple tool on a regular basis can be a reminder of what makes leaders successful and how you can continue your growth as a person and a leader. Self-reflection is always a good way to ensure you are able to achieve your personal vision, mission, and goals.

Chapter 2: Success by Design: Scholar–Practitioner–Leader

Dr. Dennis Clodi spent 32 years in public education as a teacher, principal, and superintendent. An adjunct professor for two universities since 2003, he is an expert in leadership and management, organizational change, communication strategies, problem identification and action plan development, school finance, and grant writing.

Dennis has been CEO of three successful Internet Service Provider companies serving nine rural communities. He was also President and CEO of a successful computer sales and service company. In 2003, Dennis sold these successful companies to allow more time to for him to do consulting and professional development training for companies such as UPS, Federal Express, Sears, Alberto Culver, as well as other community organizations and school districts.

An author and editor, Dennis has an M. Ed. in Educational leadership from the University of Illinois and an Ed. D. Degree from Illinois State University. With a 20-million dollar grant, he designed and delivered professional development training to over 8,000 teachers on the topic "Designing Engaged Learning Instruction and Technology Activities in K-12 classrooms."

Dennis has been an entrepreneur since the age of 13. Being a skilled ventriloquist allowed him to earn enough money to pay for his bachelor's degree. His performances on TV and Radio provided him the opportunity to travel throughout Canada, promoting tourism in America and sport fishing in Florida.

Dr. Clodi is a certified substance abuse trainer for trainers and the author of a communications manual for parents, *Mountain Education: The answer to the 3 D's—Drinking, Driving, and Drugs* is a Subject Matter Expert with Professional Progress Academy. He can be reached at d9clo43di14@btc-skynet.net

SECTION 2

Characteristics Of Everyday Leader Heroes

CHAPTER 3

The Supportive Quality in Leader Heroes

Contributed By Morris G. Nutt

"If I have seen further it is by standing on the shoulders of giants."—Isaac Newton

Support: to bear all or part of the weight, to hold up.

As it relates to leaders, support is an important quality as leaders are expected to bear the weight of an organization and to hold up the principles of why the organization was formed.

When you explore this in the traditional sense, there are numerous examples of how leaders provide support to an organization. I always look for the non-traditional to learn how innovative leadership characteristics can be demonstrated and proven effective at the highest level.

Let's explore support in the traditional sense. Most companies are built by a visionary leader and a leadership team that is focused on defining and refining profit drivers to ensure that the revenue streams are tapped and the expenses are well managed. This strategy is thought to provide long-term support, primarily financial support, for an organization.

The everyday leader hero I found has technically broken all of these rules and has taken the word support to a whole new level. Blake Mycoskie built a company on a business model of giving away half of everything the company makes. A customer purchases a pair of shoes, and his company, TOMS, gives a pair of shoes away. His vision as a leader hero is to have a positive economic and cultural impact on the world by providing the ultimate in support, shoes.

Over 40 percent of the world does not have shoes. Blake believes and has seen that with shoes, children and adults can prevent life threatening diseases and are more likely to be able to walk to work or school and to contribute to their community in a positive fashion.

Blake has proven that support can be successfully redefined by future leader heroes to have an even greater impact on the world. As a leader, he set the tone by creating a culture built around support—support in the form of people, volunteers, a product, and a culture. Blake's company culture supports the business model and has created a customer base that supports the innovative business model as well. In this situation, support is being led both internally and externally.

Support means more than just financial assistance, even if companies usually regard it as the most important component. Blake believed that financial support did not have to be structured in a traditional sense. He has boldly stated that most businesses can afford to give more if they adjusted their way of thinking from the traditional to the non-traditional.

Blake has shown the world that an everyday leader hero can be born into modest means and build an empire based upon a counterintuitive business model centered around the word support. He is a shining example of the supportive quality that is found in everyday leader heroes. After all, he believes shoes are more than a luxury; they are the support for a sustainable economy.

How Does One Learn Support?

Each day we grow with our experiences and interactions with others. There are people we meet every day that can be easily classified into categories. We meet teachers, students, bosses, employees, players, and cheerleaders, each serving a role and a purpose. There seems to be a ying to every yang, and complement to every half moon that completes the circle, bringing everything into harmony and balance.

These necessary partnerships prove in life that support systems must exist. Without support, there is no structure, no form, and no way to begin or end anything.

If a ball game takes place without spectators, did it really happen? The players need the fans as much as the fans need the players.

We are players and characters in this game of life. We need cheerleaders, band members, officials, rules, scoreboards, and of course, fans! We need support heroes. Let's explore the top characteristics of support.

Helping Others

Helping and supporting others to reach their potential is the one act that alone can help you achieve your potential and your greatness. To help someone else from a standpoint of complete selflessness, where you have no desire or intention of personal gain of any kind, is to feel pure love and is a hallmark of true leadership.

Being a supportive person to someone else and his dreams does so much more than help him or give him a warm and fuzzy feeling inside. The act itself sets in motion a domino effect of good works that is incalculable throughout a millennium.

The first support heroes that demonstrate the help characteristic are our parents. There is very little in this world that is more powerful or more permanent than the love of a parent for their child. When one thinks back on their life, they realize their mentor, guardian, or parents made an impact on their lives and significantly affected who they are today.

Parents make the largest differences with the small acts of kindness and support—a simple hug or kiss, a supportive pat on the back, or a nod or wink at the right moment, perhaps a small bit of wisdom or advice given in the midst of loneliness or despair.

"The Butterfly Effect" is a term some people use to refer to how a small act affects things from afar and into the future in a big way. An act of support is in itself wonderful in that the deed helps foster an individual or organization to a higher place or to a worthier goal. However, when considering the grander picture, it does so much more. It also tears at the walls that block us from reaching our potential, chipping away at fear, hate, anger, jealousy, envy and pride.

The domino effect of achieved through acts of support is crucial in a world full of stories of war, starvation, and violence. It is easy to see we can improve our condition by adopting more of a supportive nature. We must understand that war, violence and other negative social conditions are merely the offspring of an incorrect mindset. When people come from an inner place of lack instead of like, those negative actions crop up, giving rise to lamentable social conditions.

- How can one become more supportive and change someone's mindset from lack to like?
- How can you learn or develop the good characteristics you remember from your supportive hero?

You can accomplish this by first becoming aware of where you are in the process. Ask yourself:

- How much service do you give versus how much you expect or take?
- How often do you reach out to others to help them versus asking for help?
- In conversations, to what extent do you ensure that the person with whom you are speaking is able to voice their needs and concerns as much as you are able to do so?

Once you become more aware with your level of strength in these areas and begin practicing daily efforts in improving your supportive nature, you will begin to notice several changes starting to take place around you.

One of the changes you will become aware of is that your needs will decrease. Most of us have been conditioned to think that we need much more than we already have. Because of this mindset, we do not have the time or resources to help others. We simply believe we need more time and resources to continue to feed the imaginary monster we have created inside of our own heads—an unhealthy mindset.

As you become increasingly supportive, you begin to see all those around you who have helped support you in your efforts along the way. A feeling of gratefulness washes over, and you begin feeling more and more gratitude as you notice other "angels" who are out there helping others. It is as if a veil has been lifted, and now you can truly see what this life is really all about and what your purpose in the grand scheme of things really is, including how important you truly are.

At some point, you may feel overwhelmed by the enormity of it all. You may be stunned at your new feelings and awareness, and you may be a bit saddened that you didn't embrace this truth much earlier in life. Many will never come to know this great feeling and incredible truth. You should change as many people over to this way of thinking as you can, as this will enable you to affect multiple areas of your life as well as multiple generations into the future. You are chipping and chipping away at any potential negative consequences of a "lack" mindset. You are "paying it forward."

Trusting Others

The truth really does set us free when we come to learn that as we begin giving, especially for the first time, our needs and personal focus begin to decrease quite dramatically. We start realizing we are accomplishing more, not less, and our focus has shifted from self to others. When we focus on others, we tap into an energy force like no other.

I have observed there is an extreme lack of trust that pervades the mindset of many. Some of this is warranted because we have had some bad experiences at the hand of others, and while we may forgive our trespassers, it is very hard to forget, move forward and treat these events as isolated cases. When this happens, an obstacle or block occurs within our mind that automatically shields opportunities from us.

As more and more blocks occur in the mind, it is like too many notes jumbled together on a whiteboard; we find less and less space for new ideas, new ways of thinking, and new people and opportunities to serve. As we become bogged down, we seem to be dismayed as to why things are not going right for us. We don't understand why life isn't flowing as easily as it was before. We are shocked at how others seem to be moving forward while we are sitting still. These feelings may then take on emotions of fear, anger, bitterness, and envy, prompting us to adopt a fight or flight response. Herein lies our challenge; herein lies a vicious cycle of which we need to break free—the good news is that we can.

"When I was a young man going through that awkward age we all go through in which we desire nothing more than to belong and be accepted, it was easy to fall into the cycle of doubt, fear, envy, and greed. I would talk to my support heroes about these challenges. They would point the way for me. They would challenge me to practice good deeds and read great books. It took me several years and the studying of many great books, like Think and Grow Rich and How to Win Friends and Influence People, before it dawned on me that what I really needed to do was to trust in the rewards of helping others.

At first, it was small stuff like smiling at everyone I passed, then it grew to complimenting others or patting them on the back for a job well done. The more good I did the better I felt, and I was making others feel very good about themselves too. I did this from seventh grade until I graduated from high school.

I remember watching award after award being handed out to others. I watched and congratulated them repeatedly. The class favorite award went to the same people year after year; so did best athlete, class president, smartest student, and so on. I was not voted any of these things until my senior year.

In my last year of high school, almost as a strange twist of fate, a few of the very popular people who won most of the annual awards and garnered most of the attention nominated me as Senior Class President. After the vote was taken, I found out I had won!

However, the awards and rewards of helping and supporting others over the previous years didn't stop there. I was also blessed to be voted president of my high school Future Farmers Association (FFA) Chapter. I represented the Future Business Leaders of America (FBLA) in speaking contests, was selected to represent the State of Arkansas as a National FFA president candidate, and was voted by my senior class as one of several class favorites.

It was quite the watershed year, and it was the boost of confidence I needed as I headed into my college years. There were other great awards and rewards garnered that year, but the true reward was how a very fractured class of different personalities and interests in the seventh grade had come together to graduate as a close group of friends.

We, as a class, were referred to by our high school principal as "the best class to come through this school that I can remember." It was quite the compliment to our class, and it came as the result of many of us applying the principles of being supportive as set forth in this chapter."

- Morris Nutt

These principles work just as well in the adult world as they do in our formative years. The key is being aware of them and practicing them on a daily basis until they become habits. Then, each day, you become just as concerned with your fellow man as you are with yourself. Therein lies one of the greatest success secrets in life.

Every step along the journey is lit by the love of a supportive leader hero. Make no mistake; you will have your share of challenges, but knowing there are support heroes all around you will make your journey easier and less daunting. This is just one of the reasons why we must acknowledge, validate, and appreciate our support heroes.

Finding a Why

Support leader heroes know the "why" behind what they are doing. It is often a daunting task to be in a supportive role day in and day out, especially when you are leading a large organization, a massive team, an entire family, or a country. In studying successful leader heroes, I found that each of them understands why they are providing the support they are. Look at Blake. He came extremely close to winning a million dollars on the Amazing Race, but he didn't. He believes it was fortunate for him because it drove him to uncover the real why behind his life.

It was through his travels that he discovered a real passion and why for helping the less fortunate with something that many other people take for granted, shoes. The why overcame him and is the fuel that allows him to run his company and support his cause.

It is often said, "If the why is strong enough, you can figure out how." This quote should actually read, "If the why is strong enough, you can support the how," because support is the structure that allows for massive action, significant growth, and extreme impact.

Leader heroes understand their internal why. Understand what it is that drives them daily to perform at extraordinary and often seemingly impossible levels. This is the fuel that will support and sustain long-term growth.

One challenge for you is to ask yourself why you are doing what you do. It doesn't matter what your career, business, passion, or life's role. Just answer why. Go ahead, take a few minutes and write it out. As you write, you may have a flood of additional thoughts, ideas, and emotions that arise, so you may need an additional sheet of paper. Let it flow. Remember, this is your fuel you are pumping into your system for long-term sustainability.

Remember what I discussed in the beginning of this book: adopt a pioneering spirit, and know that these characteristics are like a contact sport. They take a team. The more supportive you are, the more support you will receive from those around you. You have to be willing to help others, trust the process that this giving nature will provide massive support to you, and always remain fueled by your why.

"We make a living by what we get, but we make a life by what we give."—Winston Churchill

Dr. Rich's Prescription for Success

1. Create a "helping others" journal. List the activities that you are doing to help other people every day, from family to friends to colleagues to clients to vendors in your community. List these in short sentences or bullet descriptions.

2. Make a Feeling Notation. At the end of each helping task that you did, just make a note of how you felt. When one ties feelings with actions, it is more likely to "wire" the response in your brain. The goal is to create unconscious responses so that acting in a way that supports others becomes natural to you and immediately allows you to feel good.

3. Refer to your why card every day. Add images to it to anchor in the feelings associated with it. This will assist you in developing the supportive characteristic that is important for everyday leader heroes. You will find that over time, you are fully fueled and energized. You might even surprise yourself as to how you can accomplish so much. It is because you have the ultimate abundant natural fuel, your Why.

Chapter 3: The Supportive Quality in Leader Heroes

Morris Nutt is an author, speaker, consultant, thought leader, and wealth mindset expert living in Memphis, Tennessee. He is CEO of Morris Nutt Financial, LLC. Morris enjoys traveling, reading, speaking, writing, helping others achieve their worthiest goals, and spending time with his family.

Morris co-authored *The Laws of Financial Success* with Edward Cowles and is one of the contributing authors in the new bestseller from Brian Tracy, *Counter-Attack*, for which he was inducted in the National Academy of Best Selling Authors and earned the 2011 Golden Quill Award. Morris currently has three other books in the creation process. He enjoys helping others, and his motto is, "You are destined for greatness!" For more information about Morris, visit www.morrisnutt.com

Chapter 4

The Listener Quality in Leader Heroes

Contributed By Dr. Donald Patrick Lim

"Leaders we admire are leaders who listen."
—Dr. Donald Patrick Lim

Listen: to pay attention, to make an effort to hear something

When you think of a great leader, the ability to listen comes across as a common quality, as a leader must be able to listen to the changes in the marketplace, listen to the needs of employees, customers and vendors, as well as listen to themselves.

There are many examples of how listening has been integrated into the building of successful companies and innovative products. However, it is not often that you hear of a company being built by listening to a child. Jack O'Dell built a massively successful company by listening to his daughter. It all started in 1952. Jack was a self-taught engineer who worked in a small die-cast company in London. He would see his daughter off to school each morning, and she would walk out with her matchbox in hand.

You see, her school only allowed students to bring toys to school that would fit in a matchbox. Being a creative and free spirit, Jack's daughter, Ann, would take spiders and other such items to scare her peers. She didn't much care for trying to find toys small enough to fit in the little matchbox. Plus, she thought this approach was much more fun and exciting. Well, her father didn't find it fun and exciting to continually receive phone calls from the school insisting that Ann find normal toys to bring.

Listening to the school's administrators, Jack knew he could punish his daughter—but for what? She was only honoring her quirky sense of humor and adhering to the guidelines of fitting a toy into a matchbox. Being a resourceful engineer, Jack made a small die-cast red and green steamroller, which fit nicely into the little matchbox. Since he had made it for Ann, she was proud to take it to school and didn't mind giving up her spider antics.

When Ann opened her matchbox, the other students weren't afraid anymore. Rather, they were amazed at the size of the little toy she had. It was an instant hit, and all of her friends wanted to know where they could get a matchbox car of their own. As his daughter came rushing home telling her father to make more cars for her friends, Jack listened and realized there was a demand.

Thereafter Jack began by studying car manufacturers to ensure that the cars he was building were accurate, designed to scale, and complete with all the details a perfectionist would insist upon. He created molds to die-cast the tiny parts and then built machines to assemble and paint the toys—quite an endeavor in the early 1950s given the lack of technology. He was able to manufacture these small cars quickly and inexpensively, which was perfect because they quickly caught on throughout England. The toy craze even spread to the United States as well.

Now, Jack O'Dell was born in 1920 London and was raised in a poor family. He didn't spend much time in school and was kicked out of school by the age of thirteen. He held odd jobs, and then joined the Army. When he came out of the Army, he joined a couple of friends in the die-cast factory, and they were committed to making parts for traditional cars.

By all measures, Jack was an ordinary man. However, by taking the time to listen, he became an everyday leader hero in my book. Matchbox cars are still a craze and a hot item that children today enjoy. It is interesting to me that this man, though not highly educated and not financially wealthy, had the insight to listen and fill a need. What is really interesting is that he listened to the school's demand while also listening to his daughter's heart and quirky sense of humor to set the tone for what he created. He could have easily punished her and simply demanded that she come up with something else to take to school. Instead, he listened with his heart and knew that she needed something unique that the other children would not have.

In a 1969 interview, The Daily Telegraph called Jack a "damn good engineer." I prefer to think that he was a damn good listener. This story is an excellent demonstration of how listening can lead to the building of a significant company that can endure time.

Leader heroes are listeners. It is impossible to be a leader without listening, and one can't have followers without listening. Followers are those who provide valuable input and honest feedback on how work is done and how to be more efficient. A leader who fails to listen fails to lead effectively.

How Do You Learn to Listen?

Throughout some personal journeys, five listening experts shared their secrets and wisdom for learning "how to listen." In the next few pages, you will learn these valuable steps.

Practice Physical Listening

Physical listening is all about body and mind listening. It means that one's eyes and body language focus on the speaker. It also means giving full, undivided attention so that the person speaking will feel the respect that should be given to him. If you look at it, during the times you give undivided attention and really listen, you were likely able to absorb more quickly what was being told to you and then to ask appropriate follow-up questions.

Usually, when you try to do two things at once while listening to someone, you actually move slower. Physically listening allows you to understand, contribute, and add value to the discussion immediately. When you are in this zone, you will realize that you are actually saving time, moving faster and, more importantly, giving the deserved level of respect to the person who is speaking to you.

> "One of the greatest leaders I try to emulate is my father. I have always looked p to and admired him. Coming from humble beginnings, he struggled to finish college, only to fail the government accounting licensure exam. That made it impossible for him to go into the corporate world. Therefore, he endeavored to start his own business instead

by borrowing 10,000 pesos ($200 at that time and growing turned it into a business worth millions.

One of the biggest benefits of being the son of a businessman is that I was able to see my dad more often than those with a traditional nine-to-five job. At the time my father began his business, we were renting a small three-story house. The ground level served as his office; the second floor was where my siblings and I stayed; the top floor was my parent's bedroom. I remember playing hide-and-seek around the house as a kid, oblivious to the numerous laborers and customers coming in and out of our house. My dad was the boss, so no customers or office staff could complain as we ran around the house and ground floor.

My father's path to success was not easy, and he didn't take any shortcuts. He was frugal. He kept clothes he had worn for 15 years. While he was generous with us as far as providing us with books and clothes, he was personally happy with watching Chinese movies and playing chess with his friends. Apart from that, he would always tell me, "Money saved is better than money earned." He always believed that to be rich meant to know how to save.

My dad and I never had a lot of one-on-one time because he was busy building his business. However, during times when I did have one-on-one time with him, he always gave me his undivided attention. These days, whenever I visit my parents and want to talk to my dad, he still makes sure that he is listening attentively to me. When I visit, he would usually be in his bedroom watching his favorite TV program or working. Regardless of what he is doing, whenever I come into his room, he turns off the TV, stops working, and simply asks, "What do you want to talk about, son?" It gives me this priceless feeling of knowing I am getting his undivided attention.

I have learned to appreciate how to listen attentively now that I am a professional having to deal with hundreds of people. People come to my office daily wanting to speak to me on a variety of different matters, both professional and personal. The importance is physical listening."

- Dr. Donald Patrick Lim

Realize that Silence is Golden

Oftentimes when people are together, there is a tremendous amount of pressure for constant conversation to take place. However, those who are more seasoned or those who have spent a longer time together feel no need to talk all of the time. Sometimes body gestures and eye movements are enough. And in many instances, complete silence is enough for a conversation to happen. Some people say the best soul mates do not have to talk. They can just gaze at the moonlight, hold hands, and complete a conversation by just listening to one another in complete silence. The more comfortable we are with silence, the more we observe and communicate.

> "My daughter taught me how to appreciate silence. Some time ago, I came home after a two-week business trip. I missed my daughter greatly. After giving her a tight hug, I asked her to tell me all that had happened in the two weeks that I was gone. She wasn't saying anything, so I started telling her about my stories. I kept talking and paused occasionally, asking her repeatedly to tell me her stories. Finally, she put her hand gently on my mouth and said,

> "Daddy, you don't have to keep talking to make up for lost time. Just be quiet. I just want to sit here with you and hold your hand." Her words had a tremendous impact on me. I realized that my daughter didn't want to listen; she wanted me to listen in silence."

> - Dr. Donald Patrick Lim

It is important to continually listen, even if it means listening in silence. Are you aware of when you need to listen in silence? Once you become more aware, it will be apparent, and you will be amazed at how you can hone all of your listening skills to become a better leader.

Listen With an Open Mind

Listening should come with an open mind. Someone who listens without an open mind really isn't listening at all. What good is listening when one's mind is already closed? Listening is an art. It is impossible for people to go into a conversation without their own biases, perceptions, and prejudices. Thus, listening to a person speak without revealing one's own biases through facial gestures and body movements is an art unto itself.

Many of you have been in a situation where you were the cocky young manager or where you were the one who gave an employee his job. So often, people in upper management positions instantly shoot down random, new, and fresh ideas from young managers when, in fact, it is important to keep an open mind and open heart. If you want to continue your business the same way it has always been, then continue doing the same thing. The definition that comes to mind, however, is that of insanity—repeatedly doing the same thing while expecting a different result.

When you look at the inherent quality of an everyday leader hero, they listen with an open mind. Jack O'Dell had an open mind as he listened to his daughter and her school. Do you listen with an open mind, or are you a person that has already made a judgment or decision without listening fully?

Applying an open mind and an open heart is the backbone of many companies and a key quality of an everyday leader hero. It is recommended to ask yourself the following questions when you are in a situation where someone is exploding with ideas or just exploding in general!

• **Am I present?**

In other words, are you actually listening and absorbing the words that are being said, or are you jumping to conclusions and planning your response (which is in the future)?

- **Am I listening with an open heart?**

Are you actually putting yourself in the other person's shoes and listening from their perspective with heart, compassion, and empathy? Do you understand why they are so excited or passionate about what they are saying? Get out of your head and get out of your own way.

- **Am I pausing before answering?**

Do you cut the other person off mid-sentence, or do you wait until they are finished speaking before you pause, formulate your thoughts, and then speak? Too many people cut others off and start blurting out their opinion. That means they are not listening with an open mind or an open heart. The key is to let the other person finish speaking, and then pause. Take time to formulate your thoughts and your response so that you can communicate with an open mind and an open heart.

Practice these three skills, and you will begin to see people react to you differently. Take note and continue to hone this skill. It is not a skill set that is always natural; as we mature, it gets easier, but it will require more refinement and honing.

Engage in Focused Listening

When you are listening to someone, be focused. When you are focused, you physically move as little as possible in order to absorb what is being said. Remaining focused is often challenging, as the temptation is to lean forward or to move and to jump in with answers or an opinion.

Yet a focused listener will remain still and poised, intently looking into the other person's eyes. The true test of focused listening is one's ability to repeat what the other person has just said and to summarize it, then ask the question that you believe the person is asking. That ensures you are interpreting the conversation correctly. More importantly, it shows the other person that you were a focused listener.

Practice this skill of repeating, and you will ensure that communication is clear and accurate, thus also showing the other person the respect that he deserves.

Stop Listening and Take Action

At some point after one has proactively listened and absorbed everything, one should stop listening and take action. While listening is an art and an attribute, taking action is another attribute of a leader hero, as can be seen with Jack O'Dell, who was able to listen to a certain point and then to take the necessary action to build the tiny toy cars around which he built his company.

"Knowing when to stop listening and to start taking action was a lesson taught to me by a farmer during my senior year in college. Students were required to join an immersion program in poverty-stricken areas around the community. The objective of the program as envisioned by the leaders of the university was for students to experience those who have been living below the poverty level. I was assigned to a family in a rural area. The farmer and his family warmly welcomed me. I stayed with the farmer, his wife, and their nine children for nine days.

At approximately 4 a.m., the farmer awakened me and asked me to accompany him. We spent the next four hours feeding pigs and chickens, cutting wood, trimming grass, and tilling the soil. The farmer wouldn't give me much instruction. So, the more activities I did, the worse I performed. I kept asking him to tell me how to do the tasks correctly. He continued to say little, and I continued to pour too much, too little, and to cut unevenly.

The farmer kept smiling as I muttered about the tasks he wanted me to do. I wanted everything explained to me in detail so that I could do things in the fastest way possible, which is how I was raised and taught. I was embarrassed with my poor performance on the farm and wanted to put the blame on the farmer for not explaining tasks properly to me.

Sensing my frustration, the farmer calmly said, 'You get more things done by just doing it. There's no need to keep on listening to what I say. Your ears are not doing the work. Your arms and legs are doing the work. Learn by doing. You don't need to listen anymore, just do.'"

- Dr. Donald Patrick Lim

That farmer may have lived in poverty, but he shared words worth gold for everyday leader heroes. Often, listening to a leader will only tell you so much; at a certain point it becomes a matter of doing—taking action and modifying along the way. Our world would be drastically different if we only listened and never took action.

Remember how in the beginning I spoke about perspective and the fact that leader heroes tend to have a common attribute of letting what does not truly matter slide? When you adopt the listening qualities highlighted in this chapter, it helps you maintain a perspective on your world. You begin to have a greater ability to make decisions and to take actions based upon what is important while also determining what is unimportant because you are listening with intent, purpose, and focus.

> *"When one has the feeling of dislike for evil, when one feels tranquil, one finds pleasure in listening to good teachings; when one has these feelings and appreciates them, one is free of fear."*
> *—Buddha*

Dr. Rich's Prescription for Success

1. Physically listen. Take note of physically listening. In a world that is filled with multi-tasking and massive distractions, it is time to stop doing and start listening. Start making a commitment to eliminate distractions, and listen physically to your daily conversations.

2. Silence is golden. Learning to listen in silence is truly golden. A person can hear as much in silence as he can when listening to words. Practice "being" present and listening in silence. Note how much you learn in silence.

3. Listen with an open mind. Make sure when you are listening that you don't interrupt, that you listen to everything the person is saying, and that you have an open mind. When the person is done speaking, pause, gather your thoughts, and then speak.

4. Practice focused learning. Remember that the real test of true focus is to repeat back to the person what he said and then to re-state his question. This not only ensures that you heard things correctly, it also shows him that you respect him enough to listen with focus and intent.

5. Stop listening and take action. At some point, just take action. You can hear instructions and listen to people around you, but at some point you need to realize that you can learn more and achieve more by taking action.

Chapter 4: The Listening Quality in Leader Heroes

Dr. Donald Patrick Lim is Managing Director of MRM Worldwide, the digital and relationship marketing arm of the global advertising giant McCann Worldgroup. Before McCann, he was President and CEO of Yehey! Corporation, one of the Philippines' top digital marketing holding companies. He was also President and CEO of Media Contacts Manila, winner of 2009's Media Agency of the Year, and a product of a joint venture company between Yehey! Corporation and Europe's largest interactive conglomerate, Havas Digital.

Before Yehey!, Donald was Vice President of Marketing at the Philippine Daily Inquirer. Starting as a division head and manager of classifieds, he became assistant vice president and, eventually, vice president, all within a span of three years, after doubling the revenues of the classifieds department, launching new Inquirer products, and pioneering award-winning marketing projects and promotions.

Aside from his full-time job with MRM, Donald oversees five businesses of his own and does management consulting for up and coming brands and businesses. Donald is one of only 24 Certified Professional Marketers in the country and one of the first to be awarded the Certified Entrepreneur title by the Canadian Institute of Entrepreneurship. He is a member of the technical panel of the Commission of Higher Education and has been awarded the Dr. Bienvenido R. Tantoco Sr. Professorial Chair in Marketing by Jose Rizal University. Donald has been awarded the Young Market Masters Award in Online Marketing and an honorary certified eMarketing Consultant title by the eMarketing Standards Board of Australia.

CHAPTER 5

The Caring Quality in Leader Heroes

Contributed By Susan Kristiniak

"A smile is the light in your window that tells others that there is a caring, sharing person inside."
—Denis Waitley

Caring: feeling and exhibiting concern and empathy for others.

When I look at the definition of caring, it reminds me of 1992, when an unpretentious man by the name of Henry Buhl made a significant difference that set the tone for the level of caring in our society.

At age 62, Henry had spent his career in investment banking and professional photography when he seemingly stumbled upon something in New York City. As he was walking back from a casual lunch, he recognized a man on the street. This man was approaching him, begging him for $20. Henry recognized this man as someone he had seen sweeping streets but who had been fired for sleeping on the job.

When Henry thought about this further, he realized that there were twelve businesses up and down that street that were willing to pay someone to sweep the streets. But they didn't know whom to get, nor did they have time to go find someone suitable. Being the caring leader he was, Henry went to a local homeless shelter and spoke to the executive director. He explained that he may have a job for one of the residents but that the person would have to demonstrate his ability, responsibility, and willingness to work. The director was thrilled, and Henry found a person that was willing to sweep the streets for these twelve businesses.

Thereafter, Henry returned to Soho and found yet another block that needed sweeping. When he went back to the director of the shelter, he was greeted with open arms, even hailed as a potential hero. Henry ended up creating the Soho Partnership, which was dedicated to providing employment readiness training and job placement to New York City's recovering homeless individuals through community improvement projects. The project became known as Project Comeback.

Henry Buhl turned the program into so much more than just street sweeping. He incorporated graffiti removal, tree trimming, and snow removal in the winter. Henry cared so much that of the $6 per hour that each person was paid, 85 cents went into a Chase bank account created for them. The whole purpose was to ensure that the person would have enough money for a down payment on an apartment after graduating from this program.

Not everyone graduated, but over 70 percent did. And today, it is the caring quality that Henry Buhl demonstrated that people remember. As an everyday leader hero, he showed that he cared enough about the homeless people to lead them to a new program that would assist them in achieving true independence. That's a real demonstration of caring when there is nothing to gain personally, just a caring heart and a desire to lead to greatness.

Leader heroes create caring experiences. Caring should begin at the moment of conception and should be put into practice by our parents after we are brought into the world, swaddled in warm blankets, and celebrated. We continue to increase understanding of the concept of caring as we are nurtured through our early years. Young people are taught about caring and see it being modeled by parents, teachers, and adults who demonstrate love, kindness, and compassion. For instance, kissing a hurt finger, helping to put on a jacket, and holding a small hand teaches children about caring at an early age.

Caring is something that develops as we learn to practice our caring thoughts. Caring thoughts foster feelings for others and become a fulfilling and rewarding experience. Since we share the world with others, we have the responsibility to show our kindness and compassion for those with whom we come into contact. We seek out caring experiences in times of celebration and sadness, and we recognize that actions of caring give us an internal balance. How we demonstrate our caring behaviors and thoughts to people we meet defines who we are.

There are several aspects of caring that we will cover in this chapter for you. These will help guide you to understand the specific aspects of caring leadership qualities.

Be sure your vessel is full before giving to others.

The idea of caring can be lost in the role definition of leadership. The energy and passion of caring leaders should be focused on meeting the needs of others. Caring leaders must concern themselves with staff, customers, vendors, and other people around them.

Leaders need to recognize and attend to their own needs. The intention of healing others in a caring experience must begin with self-care practices. Self-reflection, a review of the day-to-day experiences along the path of one's career, allows one to revisit their emotional needs and to revitalize themselves. Understanding the journey of leadership, its challenges, and rewards solidifies one's ability to heal, care, and provide kindness not just to others but also to oneself.

Demonstrate Caring in Your Actions

Reflecting on caring experiences can help understand the caring hero. Henry Buhl demonstrated his ability to be a caring leader hero through his actions. He didn't ask someone else to look into the problem. Rather, he stepped up and gave a hand up, not a handout. That is how you demonstrate caring through actions.

> "I have had many memorable experiences with caring moments in my three decades of nursing. One of my first nursing positions was in a community emergency room. One specific night shift found me holding the head of a young accident victim who began to vomit as I attempted to stabilize his neck while others were rushing in to stabilize his life. My shift leader saw in me the terror I was experiencing as a new nurse working with a major trauma victim who was dying in my hands. My shift leader, a caring leader, took the patient's head from my hands, thus allowing me to step back and rebalance myself. Her act of caring and not ridiculing my inexperience saved my career.

The imprint of the trauma before my eyes could have driven me from the profession in fear and failure. No one in the room of highly skilled trauma care providers seemed to realize the importance of the action hidden in the team's attention to urgent care delivery. However, I did realize how important the team leader's caring gesture was. Days later, I acknowledged her kindness to me and told her how much her caring leadership was appreciated."

- Susan Kristiniak

Create Caring and Meaningful Experiences for Others

Personal acknowledgement of experiences represents caring in leader heroes. Many efforts of others go unnoticed, unappreciated, and unloved; leaders must account for customer satisfaction. The acknowledgment of good work can be lost in the complaints of families feeling loss of control during the chaos of a family illness. Thus, caring leader heroes must remember to celebrate positive experiences rather than just reprimanding deficiencies in performance.

Henry Buhl created a meaningful experience for the homeless by providing them with a job, a sense of pride, increased confidence, and a level of knowingness that someone truly cares. The caring experiences that he created were interpreted and remembered differently by each individual, but what's important is that they were remembered. Each person he touched and helped had a unique memory because of Henry and his acts of caring as a leader in creating a movement through a seemingly simple program.

Acknowledge the Struggle of Others and Intervene

Leader heroes who show concern, compassion, and authentic feelings for others are caring heroes. Caring heroes recognize that life occurs outside the workplace. Technology and electronic connections keep everyone informed from minute to minute, adding to the celebrations and stressors of life. Many hours each week can be spent listening to the team, the customers, and those around you. Being understanding and compassionate and openly showing that one cares for others in a personal and business environment will mean the critical difference between fleeting and lasting success. This is because lasting success is built upon a strong foundation that begins with a genuine sense of caring for each person for who he is as a person. When it is appropriate, don't be afraid to step in and step up to offer an understanding hand. That's what true leader heroes do.

Looking back at Henry, we see that he acknowledged the struggles of others and chose to step up and intervene. He chose to demonstrate the caring leader hero quality that many have inside yet don't always demonstrate. He did. His intervention has now created a positive impact on thousands of lives in New York City.

Understand the Uniqueness of Each Individual

Leader heroes balance the demands of leading and the expectations of the business in their roles to create caring environments that develop, mentor, and challenge the capabilities of those they lead. We have all experienced the leader whose efforts and energy are lost and depleted in the rigor of administrative affairs to maintain a business flow. This type of leader fails to develop passion and energy. Lost in their own functioning and contrast, the leader hero stretches and embraces the entire staff to grow and improve caring practices with him. The energy produced in this kind of caring leader hero becomes contagious and drives the team to greater success.

Understand How to Experience a Caring Leader

Experiences with a caring hero will always remain implanted in your thoughts. The special acts of compassion, empathy, kindness, and authenticity in these leaders' behaviors alert others to the power of caring and the pure acts of humanity that fill both givers and receivers. The sharing of compassion drives others to respond and react. To create a culture of caring, leader heroes must share, live, and act accordingly.

Caring seems innate, so why is it not always present? The mere act of talking doesn't give rise to proper communication; hearing is not always listening, and behaviors are not always caring. A caring act requires thoughtfulness and heartfelt intention. The emotional component, the intention and the heart of the message in one's behavior, separates caring behavior from mere acts.

We all have the unique opportunity to touch others emotionally in every act. Why don't most people? Leader heroes who care are attentive to this power. They realize the benefit of being a caring leader. While leaders cannot always meet all people's needs all the time, at least the intention of providing caring leadership will be recognized.

Are You a Caring Leader?

Reflecting on your own behaviors may help identify caring behavior practices. Sigríður Halldórsdóttir named five basic modes or categories of caring that describe behaviors and outcomes. While her model was developed specifically to describe the act of caring within the nursing industry, the model can be adapted to any leader reflecting on their own interactions with others.

Review the descriptions of the five modes and reflect on your own personal actions and behaviors. Your behaviors may not be exactly as described, but this can serve as a means of realizing the benefits or risks involved with such behaviors. Consider not only your own caring mode, but reflect also on past leader experiences and those who may have displayed these descriptions. Lastly, see how you rank on this scale.

Mode	Behaviors of Leader
Type I	1. Making others dependent
	2. Using manipulation and coercion
	3. Using humiliation
	4. Being indifferent to the person as a being
	5. Transferring negative energy
Type II	1. Dominating and controlling
	2. Finding fault
	3. Treating others as a nuisance
Type III	1. Being detached from the true center of others
	2. Exhibiting a lack of interest, insensitivity

    3. Lacking mutual acknowledgement

Type IV   1. Using kindness and concern
          2. Protecting life, relieving suffering
          3. Supporting positive energy
          4. Supporting the dignity of the person

Type V   1. Showing generosity and compassion
          2. Serving as a life-giving presence
          3. Restoring well-being and dignity
          4. Perceiving experience as "being with"
             and not "doing to"

A caring leader would ideally be a Type IV or V on this chart. These heroes demonstrate heartfelt intention and compassion, which in turn encourages others to follow. While these acts may not always be recognized, personal fulfillment will occur.

"Caring for your inner child has a powerful and surprisingly quick result: do it and the child heels."

-Martha Beck

Dr. Rich's Prescription for Success

1. Caring heroes fulfill a basic act of humanity—the art not only of doing but also of being.

2. Nurses and other professionals have expectations of caring, but all must recognize the importance of self-care to have the energy to provide these experiences for others.

3. Self-reflection offers all leaders the ability to identify their behaviors and their intentionality in their relationships with others.

4. Caring leader heroes serve as behavioral models for others, leave imprints on those they meet, and mentor meaningful and mindful human relationships.

Chapter 5: The Caring Quality in Leader Heroes

Dr. Susan Kristiniak is a nursing leader in a suburban Philadelphia hospital, where she manages a palliative care department and pastoral care service. She has developed educational programming in both integrative nursing practices and pain management across the health system. The focus of her leadership includes attention to holistic care for both patients and members of healthcare team.

Susan is certified as a psychiatric nurse and as an advanced holistic practitioner. She has coordinated the design and use of a Healing Room for staff at this acute hospital site. She resides outside of Philadelphia, PA with her husband, two daughters, and two golden retrievers. Susan is a Subject Matter Expert with Professional Progress Academy.

CHAPTER 6

The Humble Quality in Leader Heroes

Contributed By Jim Murphy

"Genuinely humble leaders build winning teams by encouraging trust and confidence."—Jim Murphy

Humble: having or showing a modest or low estimate of one's own importance.

Leader heroes are humble; they have humility. Followers are drawn to humble leaders not because they possess that attribute internally, but because they display it outwardly as humility. It is that outward humility that followers find so appealing.

In spite of its appeal and despite being one of the 10 most commonly identified characteristics of good leaders, humility can be elusive. Being humble is not ingrained in modern business culture or in many other American sub-cultures where people compete, even people on the same team. In fact, to speak highly of oneself is encouraged and even looked upon favorably in some cases. It is also sometimes necessary to switch between humility and self-promotion, as when writing one's own resume or filling up an evaluation, or when asking for a raise or promotion.

Qualities of Humble Leaders

Humility is often displayed subtly and may be difficult to recognize, especially before truly getting to know a person. Humility is even more difficult to identify in new leaders. Whether a person is promoted to a position of leadership from within an organization or from outside, leaders often feel the need to promote their own abilities and knowledge to show off their superiority in an attempt to command respect. This is one of the worst mistakes a leader can make. Followers are often suspect of new leaders. Internal promotions often follow internal competition, so a new leader may be challenged.

Similarly, leaders coming from outside an organization are likely to not be trusted immediately. Very often leaders in these positions sense this challenge to their authority and attempt to exert themselves forcefully. The opposite strategy will often work better because it is less likely to offend or anger followers and will most probably actually make them feel like the new leader is simply the newest member of the larger team.

People are naturally drawn to humble leaders. The attraction to humble co-workers and subordinates is the same, and in each case, humility is an appealing attribute.

Think about how often people describe others positively in reference to their self-deprecating demeanor; it's a common compliment. Self-deprecating humor is one way people intentionally deflect admiration because they truly are humble. In some cases, it's a technique employed to make one appear humble. Whichever the case, displaying humility is an attractive attribute that makes one more appealing personally and more effective professionally.

Humble leaders are also viewed as being more honest. Since arrogant leaders have a certain reputation they feel obliged to maintain, they may be motivated to inflate their own accomplishments or ability. Conversely, humble leaders are less inclined toward such over-estimation because their self-worth and reputation are based far less on self-promotion and on maintaining an air of superiority. The humble leader will also admit mistakes more readily. As we have all witnessed with numerous politicians—most of who have reputations for being anything but humble—powerful and arrogant professionals have a difficult time admitting personal or professional failures.

Additionally, one's failings cannot be hidden. Arrogant leaders are less likely to take full responsibility and are more likely to justify their actions. Humble leaders take responsibility, face their failures, and take corrective actions.

You Can't Fake Humility

This concept is a bit counterintuitive because modern business culture and, in many ways, the broader American culture, reward aggressiveness, which is often closely tied to less humble personalities. We are all too familiar with leaders with overbearing demeanors, which is arguably much easier to identify. In spite of cultural influences, people seem to understand that being humble is attractive, even those who don't necessarily possess the attribute. Unfortunately, those who understand it but don't possess it may attempt to fake it. Like any other quality, faking it won't work.

Humility is generally a character attribute learned over time. Even those who purposefully decide to be more humble will find that becoming so is not as easy as deciding to be so. Initial attempts to exude humility may prove unsuccessful if one is not genuine in the attempt. Subordinates are smart and will detect false humility. To make matters worse, such display of insincere humility may be even more off-putting than arrogance. At the end of the day, leaders must be sincere in their desire to be humble.

Why Some Leaders Lack Humility

Many leaders fail to be humble for one of three reasons. Understanding these causes should help leaders reflect on their own level of humility. The ability to identify these causes in subordinate leaders can help in mentoring them to be more effective leaders and followers.

Some leaders who fail to demonstrate humility genuinely have an elevated opinion of themselves. These types of people are difficult to change because their sense of self is so strong that it negatively affects their ability to open themselves to suggestions from others. Opening oneself in that way requires one to be somewhat vulnerable, and arrogance does not provide space for the necessary vulnerability.

The second group of leaders is made up of those who actually have a low opinion of themselves. To counter these feelings, they choose arrogance in an attempt to display confidence in the hope that others will see them in a better light than they see themselves.

The third population of leaders not only have a high opinion of themselves; they also have a low opinion of others. This group is the most destructive to an organization because they, more than other arrogant leaders, do not cultivate followership among subordinates nor among peers. In this case, these leaders and the groups they lead are unlikely to be effective.

In each case, a lack of humility can create an ineffective atmosphere across a group or organization because the leader does not appreciate subordinates' contributions and is unable to consider the honest suggestions and concerns that they raise. Sadly, in many parts of American culture, particularly in business, humility is seen as a form of weakness. This simply serves to promote such close-minded and overbearing behavior.

Consider a typical job interview, where questions about accomplishments are common. If an interviewer doesn't specifically ask about team or leadership accomplishments, job seekers are more prone to talk about individual accomplishments. Unless the hiring organization places importance on humility, responses that focus on team accomplishments make applicants appear less qualified. As a result, we reward people for individual accomplishments and self-promotion and reduce the importance placed on teams.

The Value of Humble Leaders

The truth of the matter is that displaying humility is a sign of strength. Strong leaders demonstrate personal strength by being humble and by giving respect and credit to others while deflecting it from themselves. Changing this cultural habit, especially if it is part of an organizational culture, results in increased productivity because subordinates more willingly carry out a humble leader's directions. Moreover, subordinates will provide a more sincere buy-in to the leader's goals and will be more likely to demonstrate initiatives because they know they will receive credit for their efforts.

Having a humble leader will also result in increased conformance by subordinates to other characteristics of the organizational culture. As an example, consider a factory that focuses on safety. If leaders visiting the factory floor do not follow the same safety procedures they demand of workers—which is common when the leaders see themselves as above the rules—subordinates will deem safety policies unimportant or will simply ignore them just to spite the arrogant leader. Conversely, the leader who displays humility by adhering to even minor rules will, through humility, demonstrate that all of the organization's rules and goals are important.

Humble Heroes Attract Followers

While contemplating this chapter and considering the humble hero examples in my personal and professional life, it was apparent that the leaders who are most impressive and towards whom we are most drawn have in one way or another displayed humility. In contrast, when we dislike or disrespect a leader, that person usually has displayed arrogance.

Early Leader Heroes Set the Stage

The appeal of humble leaders is partially natural and often the result of the earliest leaders we admire, view, and are exposed to early in life.

> "Like most young boys, my father was the first and most important leader to make an impact on my life. He not only came from humble post-Depression beginnings, but he has remained humble throughout his life in spite of many significant accomplishments and civic contributions.
>
> My other childhood hero was my uncle, George Pleat, my father's brother. Although they do not share the same last name, they share humility as one of their defining characteristics. As a child, my father always watched World War II movies with us and would share what few stories he knew about Uncle George's service as a Navy fighter pilot. I romanticized Uncle George's service and grew fond of him during summer vacations spent with him and his family. As I grew older, I came to know that Uncle George continued to serve his country in positions of great responsibility and eventually rose to become a highly respected deputy director in the Department of Energy.

Uncle George never spoke about the war, at least not in front of me. It was a bit disappointing, but as I matured, I came to understand that many veterans don't talk about their experiences. What I learned later was that Uncle George was more humble than I could have imagined. The greatest example of this humility was found in his self-published memoir, The Journal of a Lifetime. While writing a memoir may seem like the antithesis of humility, the book was intended largely to serve as a collection of his family's history.

George Pleat did not become a national war hero, but his combat service was nonetheless important and contributed directly to the U.S. Navy's success in the Pacific campaign, specifically in relation to the battles of the Philippine Sea, Iwo Jima, and Okinawa. Regardless of any personal risk, hardship, or aerial combat achievements, Uncle George described his service in a stereotypically humble way as demonstrated in the closing sentence of his final reflection on his service:

'One last comment, a sincere one at that: No matter what… accomplishments I may have experienced in the Naval service, there were so many others that did more, suffered more and gave up more that my contributions shrink in all comparison.' George Pleat

It is important to recognize, acknowledge, and appreciate the humble leaders that surround us, impact us, support us, and lead us."

- Jim Murphy

Write the names of the three most important leader heroes in your life that demonstrate humility.
1.
2.
3.

Look for Humble Leader Examples Everywhere

Examples of humble leaders can be found in unexpected places. A humble leader is modest. He makes everyone around him feel important while downplaying his own accomplishments. Those two complementary actions make the leader and the team more cohesive and, therefore, more effective, particularly over the long term.

Humble leaders often display these characteristics in subtle ways, but subtlety in this area commonly reflects genuine humility, and being genuine is important. Attempting to display a positive leadership characteristic that one does not truly possess or believe in will be noticeable to subordinates and can produce negative effects.

Whether subtle or not, the impact of humility is great. Humble heroes believe and promote that very few accomplishments revolve around one person. They understand that even their own accomplishments are the result of actions by their subordinates and peers. Even an accomplishment that might qualify as being truly individual is typically the result of some ingrained lesson learned from a mentor or teacher.

Reflecting on one's own humbleness or arrogance is not always easy. In order to truly be objective, you must strive to be neither humble nor arrogant. You must seek an objective middle ground to help you truly consider your own personality and performance. A sincere effort to reflect on your own sense of self and how you are perceived by others can be rewarding and can help you lead yourself toward becoming a more effective leader and follower.

A June 2011 Fox News article about former U.S. House Speaker Newt Gingrich's then imploding presidential campaign stated, "Americans expect people to humble themselves (or be humble) before they are allowed to lead." This quote is instructive because it highlights a leadership fact that many leaders refuse to admit: regardless of one's position and implicit authority, it is only when followers decide to allow a leader to lead that they actually and effectively can do so. Until such time the leader simply has a bully pulpit that is never as effective over the long run. Humble leaders often become heroic to followers, and it is they who earn enduring respect and who lead teams that achieve the greatest results.

> *"The most important question to ask on the job is not, 'What am I getting?' The most important question to ask is, 'What am I becoming.'"*
> *Jim Rohn*

Dr. Rich's Prescription for Success

1. You can't fake humility—highlight the experiences in your life that have made your humble. List them and then list the qualities that you possess today because of these experiences.

2. Strength is the ultimate value of a humble leader—highlight how each of the experiences you listed made you stronger. Be specific and list individual areas of your life or characteristics that are stronger. Focusing on the details is how you can increase your awareness and overall sense of gratitude.

Chapter 6: The Humble Quality in Leader Heroes

Jim Murphy served 21 years as a Spanish linguist in Navy cryptology, retiring as a Senior Chief Petty Officer in 2008. He led diverse groups of technical specialists in Signals Intelligence operations ashore and onboard U.S. and NATO submarines. His most gratifying assignments were in leadership positions, personnel management, and professional development. He has served in a variety of positions with Navy-wide impact, including the worldwide assignment of approximately 900 Navy cryptologists, global recruiting for all intelligence specialties, and career-long training for 1,700 crypto-linguists. He became a respected leadership facilitator and mentor while on active duty and has continued in that role since retiring.

In June 2009 Jim became the first author of "From the Deckplates," the only column by an enlisted professional in the 138-year history of the U.S. Naval Institute's flagship publication, *Proceedings*. He's a two-time winner of the Institute's Enlisted Essay Contest and views his role as a columnist as being an advocate for enlisted issues in the Sea Services and a vocal critic of policy and program decisions. His May 2011 column, entitled "On the Faces of Others," was described as "saying volumes … in an almost magical manner" while "explaining the foundations of leadership."

Jim holds a Bachelor of Science in Management and Human Resources from Park University and a Master of Science of Strategic Intelligence from the Joint Military Intelligence College. Since retiring from active duty, he has worked in several capacities in foreign language, regional expertise, and culture training management for the Department of the Navy.

Chapter 7

The Integrity Quality in Leader Heroes

Contributed By Nate Bloom and Erin Hopkins

"Integrity is also attributed to various parts or aspects of a person's life. We speak of the attributes such as professional, intellectual, and artistic integrity. However, the most philosophically important sense of the term 'integrity' relates to general character."—The Stanford Encyclopedia of Philosophy

Integrity: adherence to moral and ethical principles; soundness of moral character; honesty

Being a Person of Integrity

One of the questions that is often asked in business is: What is one of the most critical things one can do to be successful in business? Many might come up with answers like passion, creating a great working environment, and even developing solid relationships.

Certainly, the qualities listed above are important and are necessary to be successful. Nevertheless, the question remains, what is the most important thing one can do to become successful? There is something that needs to be placed before all of the above-mentioned qualities, something that will help your business succeed beyond your wildest dreams. With it your relationships with your prospects and clients will improve, your referrals will increase, your sales will increase, your repeat business will likewise increase, and your life will improve both in and outside of business.

The thing we are speaking about is the one thing only you can change. It is something that you control fully. It is a choice that is made daily, thousands and thousands and thousands of times, subconsciously. It is something only you can tarnish and destroy. It is something that takes years to build up and only seconds to destroy if you aren't careful. It is the foundation upon which many businesses have been built; it is very much involved with how many choose to live their lives, and it makes up everything that many stand for. It is one word, integrity.

"We once worked at a highly respectable company that was founded on some powerful core values. The company even had a Dream, Vision, Purpose, and Mission Statement. They had a BHAG (Big Hairy Audacious Goal). They had it all. We would gather as a sales team every morning and chant it aloud. With pride, we would scream it so loud that throughout the entire company the walls would shake and resound with these important principles. While most companies and their employees would not participate or maybe even get upset at all of the noise, we wouldn't even hang up the phone if we were on a call during the enthusiastic chant. In fact, we would proudly share with the person on the phone the importance and commitment to these words. We would hold the phone high and chant along with the others, sharing our passion and commitment to these words and values with everyone. It was who we were. They weren't just words; they were how we conducted ourselves in our desire to change the world, how this company was to be run and operated.

It was one of the most powerful things we employees had ever experienced in a corporate setting. In fact, it caused us all to become closer employees and friends. It caused us all to spend a few minutes and get fired up together for a great day of work. It made us feel proud to be a part of a company that celebrated its goals and values, whereas most companies only celebrate their accomplishments. It reminded us that we were part of something greater, something bigger than us, bigger than the office in which we worked.

Yes, it was annoying at times. There were definitely times when we would have rather showed up a few minutes late to work, conveniently missing the daily huddle. But overall, it was truly awesome. After a while, we stopped doing this chant. It was odd. It was our ritual, our morning pump up and hoorah. It was who we were. Eventually, fewer and fewer people would show up for it—the excitement and passion behind it wore off, and the flame fizzled out.

Why do we share this story with you? Because we both feel it is and was a great thing to do in any business. But when it died, so did the core values of the company. People became selfish and only cared about bettering themselves instead of truly caring for the company and its clients. The company started failing. Eventually it was forced to downsize, and over 10 percent of the team was laid off. The second round of layoffs came, and rumor had it that a third round would also follow.

Integrity is everything in business, especially today. It is a critical component in who you are as an entrepreneur or businessperson, and it is a critical component in who you are in your daily life. It is not an easy thing to do, but it is the most critical. It may cost you deals and money, but it will bring you greater success and will vastly improve every relationship that you have!

When we started our company, we founded it with very humble beginnings. We founded it with a goal in mind, with a dream of what we wanted to create, with a plan of action in place, and with integrity as our foundation. We were going to be authentic to who we were as people. We were going to represent ourselves in a way in which we could be proud, in a way that represented us as human beings.

We would be lying if we said that this didn't cost us thousands and thousands of dollars in sales, but in return for giving up some monetary possessions and money, we kept the end goal in sight and kept a strong focus on our founding values and the overall bigger picture. We turned down working with some very powerful clients and walked away from some extremely large deals because the person or business lacked our core vale, integrity.

The outcome? We have created a million-dollar business in less than a year, and our client list is such that it would even shock the best of the best (most of whom are actually our clients).

This is not a byproduct of dumb luck, nor is it a result of the gathering of some brilliant business people who have had years and years of experience and who have ran multimillion dollar companies in the past. This isn't like Donald Trump, who started with $200 million. We were just normal people with normal financial problems and normal daily struggles.

In fact, during the start-up of our company, we were broke. We put it all on the line and invested everything we were and had into a dream. We were going to be successful; there was no other option for us. We built our business from the ground up with integrity as our foundation, which created the perfect recipe for success.

When we talk about integrity and authenticity, when we say it needs to encompass everything in your life and business… we mean it."

- Nate Bloom and Erin Hopkins' Business Model and Plan

Every company needs to be founded with a vision, mission statement, a dream, and a purpose. You have to have a set of core values. These will act as a blueprint for your whole operation. These will represent who you are. And, most importantly, they must not just be words on paper. They cannot just be something you chant each morning. The core values must be something you are going to live by, things that, come hell or high water, you are never going to disregard or bend on. These are written in stone and will make up who you become as a businessperson and entrepreneur.

Branding

Integrity and authentic need to be laced throughout your branding. Make sure your branding—your logo, tagline, catchphrases, colors, web site, and social media—are truly consistent with your business and with who you are as a person. Do not mislead or misrepresent who you are and what your company represents. Remember, people do not wish to connect with a company. They want a face. They want you. You aren't selling widgets or a service. You are selling you.

Marketing

Marketing is the key that will unlock incredible success for you in your business. It is also the most difficult thing to do and by far the most overlooked aspect in almost every business. At the same time, it is the easiest thing in the world for your potential clients, buyers, and your prospects to see through. Think about it. How easy is it to spot a fake or a fraud? We see them all the time. People and businesses try to be something they aren't day in and day out.

People and businesses often represent themselves to accommodate how prospects and future clients would like to perceive them. If you misrepresent yourself, or if you market your business in a way that is not authentic, you might get some sales. Sure, you might appeal to some people who fail to see through to the real you, but we can promise you that these types of clients will be worth a quick buck to you and may help you pay your bills for the month, but they will not be loyal. Once you misrepresent yourself in your marketing and try to be something you aren't, you are done. Your clients will not follow your work, buy other products from you, or refer anyone they know to your business.

You enter into a buy-and-die relationship with everyone with whom you will do business. Some will buy from you, and then they will be dead to you. You will have burned them. They will then see right through you. These types of clients will hurt your reputation and cause more headaches and drama than the quick buck they paid you.

There are hundreds of successful people that possess integrity. Yet many have been scammed, burned, and taken advantage of, and the number of these people increases every day. The problem is that we have seen and are seeing more "wannabes" and "fakes." We live in a society that wants things now. We are all very impatient and have conditioned ourselves accordingly.

It is easy to lose sight of integrity because it is harder and takes longer to operate in a way that upholds it, yet, at the end of the day, cutting corners is dishonest. Having integrity will allow you to build rapport and trust in the marketplace. Rapport is everything. It is like a credit score in life and in your financial world. It takes a long time to build it up and a few wrong choices to tear it down.

Benefits of Integrity

Imagine a business with the integrity to put in the hard work and effort to develop a product or service that truly benefits the consumer with no lies, half-truths or fluff. In what ways do they benefit?

- Minimal charge-backs and returns—People who love what they bought because it is valuable to them don't return to businesses with complaints.
- Referrals from satisfied clients—If you have ever purchased (or, not purchased) something online as a result of reading a review, you understand the power of referral business. Asking for a referral from a satisfied customer is one of the easiest ways to get new sales.
- Repeat business—Giving people the best equates to a database of loyal fans who are likely to purchase again or who will be more amenable to up-selling efforts. Clients who avail of bigger-ticket

items or more comprehensive services mean more revenue and more profit.

- No one is selling snake oil—When a company is proud of what they have built, it shows. This image of integrity is priceless in a world full of skeptics.

Think back to a company that failed to live up to your expectation or to deliver after the sale was final. If this company lacked the integrity to make the situation right, how did you react? Many people choose to react by warning others or complaining outright about their experience. Think about this when you decide whether to make integrity a core value of your business. Research shows a customer who has had a bad experience will, on average, tell 10 people about it.

Far-Reaching Impact

The implications of a lack of integrity can escalate even further in an online world. Social media can be a company's best friend or its worst enemy; it is an outlet for people to speak their mind for the entire world to hear, which can be disastrous. If a company's integrity falters, instead of telling 10 people about a bad experience, online communities give people the chance to tell thousands about their experience.

Even if you consider yourself a person of integrity, it is important to remember that we all falter. That is why it is imperative to surround yourself with a circle of people who will keep you honest and who share the same values as you do. Maybe you remember your parents making sure you didn't hang out with the wrong crowd. Maybe you are a parent who ensures your children are associating with others who are a positive influence.

It is amazing how much we learn from others in our journey through life—both good and bad. Surrounding yourself and your business with people who share your values helps ensure honesty and integrity are a part of your everyday life.

Just as important as it is to depend on others to stay honest, it is also critical for you to help others stay honest by doing everything you can as a business owner to avoid putting others in tempting situations. Obviously, it is impossible to control the actions of others, but by putting checks and balances in place, you can help make sure this doesn't happen.

Integrity Takes a Team

If you currently run a business or plan to do so, you understand you can't do everything and do everything well. You will have to rely on the competency of others to find success. Maintaining your integrity with employees, subcontractors, clients, partners, and any other people with whom you find yourself doing business is key to success.

Never expect others to do something that you yourself would not do. Having integrity as a leader means rolling up your sleeves and getting down to it when necessary. Walk your talk. If you said you would do it, then do it. If you tell someone you will have the report done by Wednesday, finish it by Tuesday. If you promised someone a raise in 6 months, then pay it within that time period. If the meeting starts at 8 a.m., then be there before 8 a.m. and show people you respect them and their time. Breeding an environment of honesty with your internal people will shine through to your leads, customers, and your overall image. Who doesn't want to do business with a company they trust?

It seems that the online world has taken the handshake, smile, and most of the personal relationship out of sales. It has become much easier to overlook or ignore customer interactions, especially when they are not positive ones. An online company that has the integrity to deal with each bit of customer feedback, good or bad, is the company that embraces the personal relationship with the consumer, resulting in a profitable and long-lasting relationship. One of the biggest mistakes an online business can make is hiding behind a computer when times get rough.

In a brick-and-mortar world, it is easy for a customer to provide instant feedback on their experience, giving the business owner the opportunity to solidify a good experience or to fix a poor one. In a brick and mortar business, there is no place to hide. When a customer is dissatisfied, don't avoid them. This is a huge mistake. Most of the time, they want to know someone cares that they are upset. As a business owner, it is your job to figure out what you can do to "make it right" for that customer…then actually go and do it.

With you as a leader of integrity and honesty you will no doubt find massive success. This brings up the last and maybe the most important aspect of running a successful business. This final key will be the legacy of your business and the mark you leave on the world long after you are gone.

Give Back

With great fortune and success come a great opportunity and a tremendous responsibility to help those who are less fortunate. Even before your wallet is full, it is time to share the wealth. With the same passion you have for your business, find a cause that is important to you, then give, give, give. Be it a children's hospital, homeless shelter, or other charity, donate your time, money, or both, and give back to the world that has allowed your business to thrive.

It's all about helping others. Although embracing integrity in your business sometimes means turning away lucrative deals, it will more often than not lead to incredible opportunities by "paying it forward." Many times it is not about the money at the end of the day; it is about what you will gain in the long run. Not every deal you do has to be based upon profit. Paying it forward can cultivate strong, long-term relationships that can help skyrocket a business.

By helping others and expecting nothing in return, a business can achieve a level of success that many can only dream of. Many truly discover the power of the law of reciprocity, and for those unfamiliar, it is an "I'll scratch your back if you scratch mine" mentality. When you give and expect nothing, it is amazing what the universe can yield.

Help those around you get what they need and require nothing in return, then watch what happens. It could take some time, but it will come full circle—it always does—and you will be blessed with tremendous success.

Having integrity is certainly not always about being perfect. Integrity is a journey, not a destination. It is something that takes effort on a daily basis to maintain both personally and professionally. Just like entrepreneurship, it is a tough road. It is a road less traveled, but that is why it is the most rewarding. All good things come to those who work to achieve them. Nothing of true significance or value comes free in this life.

"If you are willing to do only what's easy, life will be hard. But if you are willing to do what's hard, life will be easy."—T. Harv Eker

Dr. Rich's Prescription for Success

Integrity is a critical part of running a successful business. How do you show it, and how do you know if you have integrity? Ask yourself the following questions:

1.   Are you the same person inside the business as you are outside of the business?

2.   Would the people you work with view integrity as a core value of the business?

3.   How do you handle dissatisfied customers?

4.   Do you consistently meet your commitments (appointments, tasks, financial obligations, etc.)?

5.   Do you surround yourself with other people who keep you honest and who do not tarnish your reputation?

6.   Are you able to admit when you are wrong, to do everything within your power to "make things right," and to learn from your mistakes?

7.   Does your business support a charitable cause?

Chapter 7: The Integrity Quality in Leader Heroes

Nate Bloom, an Arizona native, grew up as an entrepreneur with his father, the worldwide famous custom painter and Hot Rod builder Denny Bloom. He stands seven feet tall and grew up with a love for business and basketball. He has been an entrepreneur since age 8 and has been virtually obsessed with all things in business ever since.

Nate graduated from Mountain View High School in Mesa, Arizona in 1999 after winning a state championship in basketball. He attended Southern Utah University on a full basketball scholarship studying business and has played professional basketball all over the world while also partnering with his father to create one of the world's top Hot Rod shops and custom paint shops. Having lived in Argentina, Mexico, and Tokyo, Japan for several years at a time, Nate is fluent in Spanish and conversant in Japanese.

In 2007, Nate made a career change from basketball to the Internet, working for Infusionsoft, a highly sophisticated software company with some very respectable clientele. After working for Infusionsoft for several years, Nate combined his love of entrepreneurship and technology with his Internet marketing knowledge to help fledgling businesses succeed. Nate has helped hundreds of businesses succeed in the Internet Marketing realm. He knows the entrepreneur, he is an entrepreneur, and he can help any entrepreneur achieve their goals and reach the highest potential possible.

Nate loves people and prides himself in helping other people realize the same dreams he has been able to. He has traveled all around the world speaking to entrepreneurs at highly respected conferences and seminars. He has worked with some of the most respected business minds, speakers, and authors in the world, helping their businesses and growing their profits exponentially. He is a hard worker who gets his drive and motivation from his young son Parker.

Erin Hopkins graduated from Indiana University with a Bachelor's degree in Business and Marketing. After moving to Phoenix in 2003, she worked in various aspects of business and marketing. Erin worked as the Director of Business Development of a third party logistics company for several years then made a choice to get into Internet Marketing. She also worked for Infusionsoft in Arizona, mastering not only the product but also gaining the experience and knowledge necessary to successfully market any business. Erin has spoken all over the world sharing her knowledge and expertise, enabling entrepreneurs to grow businesses both online and offline. She has project management experience, sales force management, Internet marketing experience, and a decade of personal sales experience that give her the business savvy to increase anyone's revenue. As an entrepreneur, Erin utilizes her own experiences with internet marketing and business to guide other entrepreneurs through the process of developing a successful business in today's online world. Erin Hopkins and Nate Bloom founded AutoMarketing Pros LLC in 2010 to help entrepreneurs develop websites and automated marketing to increase revenues, repeat business and referrals. They have since helped hundreds of businesses realize success in the internet marketing realm.

CHAPTER 8

The Knowledge Quality in Leader Heroes

Contributed By Dr. Mark Vandermark

"Knowledge is power, enthusiasm flips the switch."
—Anonymous

Knowledge: possessing or exhibiting awareness in career, spirituality, mind, body and other life matters; insightful; demonstrates wisdom and passion for ongoing learning; well-informed, discerning

In this chapter it is important to shift your way of thinking about what it means to be knowledgeable. Knowledge in and of itself is irrelevant. Philosophers have been reminding us through the ages that the more we learn, the less we know. If what they suggest is correct, we are caught in a downward, paradoxical spiral. Ultimately, to know everything is to know nothing.

There is a different perspective. Instead of suggesting a knowledgeable person know this or that about a subject, it is more important to recognize how a person has learned. You have learned to notice how you think—your intrapsychic process—and how you think to the same degree as "what" you think, you begin to master the process of noticing what is going on in the world around you. This is referred to as PA, process aware. As you become more PA, you adapt and change in order to get what you want. As you change, your new experience is retained in the brain and referred to as knowledge. Becoming knowledgeable at any given time about any given subject is the result of a process of something happening to you in life.

Content and Process

Content and process refer to the "how" of life verses the "what" of life. It is fascinating to watch how people interact with each other without being aware of *how* they are doing it. In the language of professional psychology, the *way* people interact with each other is called process. The process of interaction is the how portion of being in contact with others. The topic of the conversations we have, what we are talking about, is called content.

Throughout conversations we experience both content and process. For example, you notice someone's body language or the tone of their voice. Why is it that you can talk about the same topic with one person and the conversation is brief, yet in speaking with another person regarding the same topic, the conversation goes on and on? Why are some of our conversations more pleasurable with some people, but not so with others?

The next time you are in a conversation, try to take note of both content (what you are talking about) and process (how you are both talking about it). As you talk to the other person, notice whether he or she makes eye contact, pauses to allow you to have your say, asks questions, becomes emotional, or is easily distracted away from the topic at hand. Who takes more time, says more words?

Now, take this experiment one step forward and see if you can notice the same about yourself, what you do and how you show up in the conversation. You might even ask the person if he notices the process of your conversation. Try commenting on what you notice about the conversation. As you learn to draw attention to the process, significant changes will occur.

Making the Shift from Content to Process

Waking up to the content to process shift means awakening to the processes of your life, to learning and habituating the ability to shift your attention between what you are doing and how you are doing it. Content and process participate in each other, as in the Mobius Strip, where both sides are the same side. Trace one side of the Mobius Strip, and after you complete one trip around the loop, you will notice you are on the other side of the strip itself. What appears to be a two-sided strip is only one. Similarly, content and process are paradoxically separate yet not separate.

Those who master the ability to consciously shift their attention from what they are doing in the moment to how they are doing it are those who have experienced what we call becoming knowledgeable. At this point, you will have developed the ability to shift your attention from content and process at the precise moment when doing so is crucial to getting what you want out of life.

Developing the ability to notice the process to content shift requires mastering awareness as well as noticing and discerning what you experience in life as content (what is occurring) from process (how it is occurring), and how to change your behavior based on what you notice.

Many people fail to notice their process and its impact on others. To become knowledgeable, you must wake up and notice what is occurring (here and now) as it relates to what has captured your attention in the first place. If you want to become more knowledgeable about career success, for example, you must begin by noticing your here-and-now process related to your career. If you want to change something about yourself, you must begin by becoming aware of the self you want to change. Doing so is the nature of the content to process shift.

For example, changing your career from what it is now to what it will be later requires you to notice what it is now. In other words, if you are unaware of the process of you in a career now, you have no foundation from which to refer when contemplating you in a career later. Waking up to process provides the insight and wisdom needed to evaluate your life from a different perspective. Do you want to change your spiritual life? What is the content and process of your being spiritual now? What is the content and process of your leading and influencing now? These examples illustrate the point. Knowledge is a function of becoming process aware. As you become aware of your process habits in life, they wake you up to what you must do to make the needed changes in your life to get what you want.

How to Wake Up the Process

Many people will often ask:

- How does somebody wake up?
- How do I become more process aware?
- How do I shift my attention from content to process?

The answer lies in four simple words: respond to powerful questions. Yes, that's it. Respond to powerful questions. Keep in mind that responding to a powerful question may not be as easy as it seems. Waking up can be challenging. It's one thing to ask, read, or answer a question, but it is something quite different to respond to a powerful question. That may not be as easy as it seems. Waking up can be challenging as well. It's one thing to ask, read or answer a question, but quite another to respond to it.

Responding to a question means taking the question seriously, discussing it with others, and devoting the time to think critically about what it means to you. Doing so requires process awareness thinking. You must learn to create a new inner dialogue—you talking to you about you. Ultimately, responding to powerful questions leads to taking action. Genuine process awareness responses to powerful questions will change your life.

A genuine process aware response requires disciplined self-talk that will guide your actions into a new direction that makes a lasting change, a process habit change. It requires you to notice, to learn, to commit, and to change. Those who ponder powerful questions and eventually dismiss them will remain non-process aware, which means they continue to lack knowledge regarding critical areas of their life. Dreams remain vague, relationships may crumble, and financial well-being may even diminish. Everything seems to go wrong, and there often seems to be no way out.

Powerful Questions

Becoming process aware relies on your ability to answer powerful questions, and below you will find the top 20 questions that have been assembled to challenge you, push you, and ultimately help you change your life when you answer them. Read each question carefully and notice your reaction, then devote time to responding in the manner previously described. You may find it useful to contemplate your answer and then discuss it with a friend, colleague, or personal coach. Remember to choose a person that is process aware so that you are aligned in your conversation.

Give yourself appropriate time to answer these questions and take advantage of this as an opportunity for a wake-up call of your own. As you are moving from one question to another, notice your inner dialogue and your process, and remain process aware. Take note of what you are feeling. Are you comfortable? Surprised? Are you passing some questions by just to get to the next question? Are you taking the questions seriously?

There is no right or wrong answer to this process; it is just an awareness to your internal dialogue and your personal reaction. The natural tendency for most is to pay attention to the content, the question itself. But challenge yourself and shift your attention from the content to how you react when you read the question.

Are you remembering a conversation with someone else, recalling a time or situation in the past?

Also, as you read each question, take note and see if your inner critique shows up. That's the internal negative voice that usually diminishes you and talks negatively towards you. Just by reading this chapter, you will not be changed for life. That is unrealistic. However, if you complete the chapter, complete the questions, and then start to notice you are more process aware, then you are well on your way to lasting life change.

Finally, the mental process habit required for this exercise may sound strange, but strive to be you observing you as you have a conversation with yourself. What you give is what you get. The universe returns to you in like kind.

> "I recall working with a client who responded to this question: 'Regarding self-care and well-being, what do you want?' He was 95 pounds overweight and completely non-process aware to the real reason why. While he certainly understood he was taking in too many calories, he was unaware of his inner dialogue and how he prevented himself from getting healthier.
>
> He blamed his condition on as many excuses as he could muster—no time to exercise, DNA, family

genetics, thyroid problem, wife cooking unhealthy meals, too much junk food around, lack of will power, aging, and the list goes on. His wake-up call was his shift of attention from the content of his excuses to the process of making them up in the first place. He noticed his inner dialogue and how he talked himself into junk food and out of exercise. He finally noticed how he talked to himself, how he rationalized and made up excuses. As he placed more attention on his process, his inner dance, he let go of his attention on the content. Stated simply, he completed a content to process shift.

It worked. He became serious about that one area of his life. He woke up. I am happy to say that he responded fully to the question. Now, 100 pounds later, he remains gratified by his wake-up call."

- Dr. Mark Vandermark

Powerful Key Questions

Home & Personal

1. Regarding love, sex and attraction, what do you want?

2. Regarding money and freedom, what do you want?

3. Regarding energy and vitality, what do you want?

4. Regarding spiritual development, what do you want?

5. Regarding home and comfort, what do you want?

6. Regarding your relationship with your significant other, what do you want?

7. Regarding your relationship with members of your family, what do you want?

8. Regarding self-care and well-being, what do you want?

9. What process habits do you need to change right now?

10. What is the decision you have been avoiding?

Workplace

11. In your role at work, what do you want?

12. Regarding your relationship with your boss, what do you want?

13. Regarding your relationship with coworkers, what do you want?

14. What do you want out of your career in the long run?

15. What work opportunities do you have now?

16. What do you need to do in order to reach your career goals?

17. Which workplace process habits of yours do you need to change?

18. When working, where do you limit yourself?

19. Where are you asleep at the wheel?

20. What do you expect of yourself?

Reflection

Take time for reflection. Reflection means to think about your thinking or, in this situation, to analyze and make judgments about your reaction to the powerful questions. Think back to your reaction. Are you satisfied now with your response, then? How do you feel now, in this moment, as you are reading this chapter? Are you curious, bored, or still interested? As you reflect on your experience with the powerful questions and your decision about responding to them, recall how you came to your judgment of the exercise altogether. In so doing, you become even more process aware; you shift from content to process and back again. If you have noticed your ability to do so, you will continue to do so in many areas of your life.

> *"Reflection is the Crockpot of the mind. It encourages your thoughts to simmer until they are done." Anonymous*

Dr. Rich's Prescription for Success

- Knowledge by itself is irrelevant. Ultimately, to know everything is to know nothing. As a knowledgeable person, you learn to notice how you think. Doing so is becoming process aware.
- Pay attention to the process of living.
- Wake up to the content-to-process shift and awaken to the processes in your life. Awaken to learning and habituating the ability to shift your attention between what you are doing and how you are doing it.
- As you become aware of your life process habits, they wake you up to what you must do to make the needed changes in your life to get what you want.
- When you notice the process, you become more knowledgeable and, therefore, you get what you want.
- To become process aware, respond to powerful questions.
- Strive to observe yourself as you have a conversation with yourself.
- What you give is what you get.

Chapter 8: The Knowledgeable Quality in Leader Heroes

Dr. Michael Vandermark is a psychologist, speaker, author, educator, and consultant to top U.S. and international corporations. He has been working with individual and organizational clients for 22 years. He is the author of 10 publications including *Life's Wake Up Call: The Content to Process Shift*, *Wall Street & Wildflowers: Choices About Life in Corporate America*, *Spirituality in the Workplace* (with Deepak Chopra, MD), *ERA III Leadership*, and *Coaching Conversations: An Authentic Approach to Coaching in the Workplace*. Dr. Vandermark is a versatile speaker, author, corporate facilitator, and consultant. He serves four universities as a guest lecturer and associate faculty member. He resides in Scottsdale, Arizona with his wife, Lynn.

CHAPTER 9

The Motivating Quality in Leaders

Contributed By Dr. Rich Contartesi

"It's not the cards you're dealt it's how you play the game."—Anonymous

Motivation: the general desire or willingness of someone to do something.

What makes people tick? Why do some people endure insurmountable odds while others appear to give up so easily? We have all seen commercials for the Energizer Bunny©, a character for the Energizer battery, that never gives up. Remember the slogan for Timex™? "It takes a licking and keeps on ticking®."

Some people are gifted with a fortitude and innate ability to keep going so long as they haven't reached their dreams or goals. This chapter highlights how ordinary people are motivated to do extraordinary things. It doesn't matter if you were born rich or poor, and it doesn't matter what your origin or heritage. What counts is your ability to unleash the power inside of you.

You Can Do It!

As a young child, it is likely that your parents said, "You can do anything you put your mind to." This can serve as an inner candle of light during life's most difficult challenges. The popular Footprints™ poster reminds me of the same kind of endless love and support. It goes, "During your times of trial and suffering, when you only see one set of footprints, it was then that I carried you." These simple words exemplify the warm embrace of love, protection, and support most parents give their children. Their unwavering support help to build the confidence and motivation that many need to explore the unknown challenges they would face through their life journeys.

Because of a parent's support, many have never been afraid to tackle any challenge presented to them.

> "After college, my career started as a musician. I had the opportunity to perform and record with many fine musicians. Later in life, I entered the field of technology, and following more than two decades of success, I attained the position of Chief Technology Officer for a large school district.
>
> During my work career, I also found the time to further my education, obtaining a Master of Business Administration and Doctorate of

Management. When I look back on my life, I wonder how I was able to further my education while working two demanding jobs. The mantra 'you can do anything you put your mind to' was instilled by my parents and continues to resonate within me. I am an average learner with relentless motivation.

There weren't many times during life's journey when I didn't have two jobs. I would work in technology during the day and perform in bands at night. Initially, I received a bachelor's degree in music education but did not hear the calling to teach, so my passion led me to perform and travel on the road. Wow, what a whirlwind. Living the dream on the road, I traveled and performed with many accomplished musicians in wonderful venues. I met celebrities, dignitaries, politicians, and a variety of personalities I would otherwise not have been able to meet unless I had been pursuing my dream.

My dad told me on more than one occasion that he regretted not pursuing his dreams in the music industry. As a boy growing up during the Depression, he didn't have the family or monetary support to pursue his dream of being a musician. The notion of playing music was considered a frivolous luxury not afforded to poor immigrants. His immigrant parents owned a barber and beauty shop that catered to families in the neighborhood; family life was consumed working long hours to make ends meet. Home sweet home was the back of the barbershop.

My dad worked through the barriers and saved enough money to buy a used alto saxophone. There were no lessons or encouragement, just an occasional "keep it down" or "when are you going to stop sounding like a farm animal?" Still, he persevered and became an accomplished local musician. He attended a music school but had to leave after being drafted into World War II. As life would have it, music became secondary to a young growing family. Growing up, I saw Dad work two jobs and establish his reputation as a hard worker and good provider.

Dad created a strong support system for me to realize my dream. In fourth grade, my dad bought me my first saxophone. We would sit together and discuss the nuances of saxophones. He was my first music teacher, explaining and demonstrating notes and fingerings that would become the sounds of an accomplished musician. We developed a strong bond and relationship between father and son as well as teacher and student.

During high school, my summer job was to practice playing the saxophone; I didn't have a "real job" like flipping burgers at McDonald's. My neighbors were not as enthusiastic about the daily concerts emanating from my bedroom window, but that didn't bother me; I was pursuing my dream of music. In retrospect, my dad created the open and positive environment for me, the one he never had. His hard work and energy laid the groundwork for my success.

I went on to have a wonderful career as a musician. I would bring my dad to concerts or recording dates and feel his support as a parent and friend. I know in my heart he vicariously felt the success I was experiencing. My dad's student, friend, and son had achieved something through his teaching and support.

Defying the Odds

Ironically, I see many of the characteristics of my dad in my relationship with my son Richie. My son showed a propensity for football at an early age. He was strong, fast, and small, excelling on both offense and defense. He had a strong work ethic, which earned him recognition in high school as a team leader. He lettered every year and earned awards like Offensive Player of the Year and Most Valuable Player.

Soon Richie was recruited by a 1AA college in Florida and was "red shirted" his first year. A "red shirt" identifies a player who is not active to play official football games during his first year of college. Subsequently, at the end of the season, his coach was fired, and my son wasn't invited back for spring football.

He became a walk-on trying out for a South East Conference (SEC) college team and, eventually, for the team. Walk-ons are the "raw meat" a team can beat up in preparation for the next week's opponents. Over the next few years, the charm of being a walk-on football player on the scout team in the SEC quickly turned into the reality of aches, sprains, broken bones, and other nagging injuries. The two-a-day practices, film review, and weight training regiment were fueling physical and mental progress with the hope of getting a full scholarship based on hard work and associated accomplishment.

After a promising first year as a walk-on, the SEC coach was fired. A new coach equates to a new regime, and Richie was again sent back to the bottom of the walk-on promotion ladder. Being a hard worker on the field and in the weight room is important, but now, to obtain a scholarship, he'd have to grow another six inches in height. With the odds stacked against him, however, he continued to persevere.

My son was dedicated to developing all his talents and skills regardless of physical gifts and characteristics. In the film room, Richie excelled at identifying complex defenses and designing offensive routes to counterattack the defense. He continually had repetitions with the first team and demonstrated a reputation for excellent hands and route running. However, during the first year under the new coach, he logged no playing time.

During the second and third year, the hope of graduating seniors and anticipation for an expanded role was met with continued disappointment. Working hard in practice, studying in the film room, and helping the coach on a leadership role did not move Richie from walk-on to scholarship. He excelled in practice and was sought after by the defensive coaches to run plays for the following week's opposition.

Richie was asked to take an expanded role preparing the special teams and to eventually become the starting holder. As a starter, his ambition to start as a receiver was met with disappointment, yet my son never let his disappointment become a hindrance to his performance on the field nor a negative factor for his team. Richie never quit nor showed his frustration and disappointment to the team, and his positive dedication became an inspiration to other walk-ons and players.

Although his size was a detractor, Richie's spirit and love for the game prevailed. He led by example. Other players on the team sought his advice and guidance when they felt down and rejected. They saw Richie play with sprains, broken bones, and an unwavering determination to succeed. He continued to work diligently over the summer in anticipation of the final year of eligibility.

The final year would exemplify the culmination of a lifetime of practice, competition and dedication. Over the summer, the scheduled practices and depth chart began to take shape. The high hopes of being in the starting rotation were increasingly complicated with new recruits and the pressures felt by the coaches to produce.

Richie fell in the depth chart but continued to stay focused. He had been through this before, facing frustration and accepting his role on the team. He was asked to work with the new rookie place-kicker who would be facing the pressures of the hostile SEC. My son accepted the challenge and selflessly gave his all for the success of the team.

Finally, Richie was rewarded with a full SEC scholarship prior to his senior season in recognition of his personal dedication, selfless giving to the team, and inspiration for all other non-scholarship players who were hoping for a shot in Division I football. During Richie's final year, he helped cultivate the most productive kicker in the SEC and completed his dream of completing receptions during a game, all while earning the distinguished SEC Scholar Athlete Award.

It is this same hard work and dedication, learned through football, that eventually became my son's success strategy in the corporate business environment. Richie currently works for a Fortune 500 company as an account manager in New York City. The same dedication and perseverance that produced a Division I scholarship player is now encouraging others to reach their highest potential in the corporate business world. Developing a clear understanding of how frustration and disappointment can potentially debilitate an employee, Richie assists employees to take a positive, productive approach to problems in an open and safe work environment. The lessons learned during his tenure in the SEC developed a resilient character capable of guiding others through the adversity of competitive business environments."

- Dr. Rich Contartesi

Live Free or Die

Jacquie was born into the debilitating confines of communism. Twenty years after the Cuban revolution, her family was relatively well-off. Her dad, a member of the party, had secured a managerial position in a sugar cane factory. The family had food, clothing and a higher standard of living than most in poverty-stricken Cuba.

Jacquie attended primary school while living with her parents, then a secondary boarding school in another town. The repressed and distorted views of a communist-influenced curriculum and propaganda formed a negative perception of life outside of Cuba. In discussions with her family, Jaciquie's communist views, combined with isolation from the free press, painted a life of utopia in Cuba. Jacquie would continue to sing the praises of the revolution. Her family would listen intently and show support for the enthusiastic teen while recollecting what life has been like before the revolution.

Before long, Jacquie completed her secondary studies and began studying in college to become a teacher. Her outgoing personality attracted the attention of both teachers and friends. She was frequently selected to lead groups that supported the communist way of living. However, things began to change when she met her future husband George.

George's path through adolescence was opposite of Jacquie's. George started life in poverty; his family did not share the luxury of a charmed communist existence. His large family sustained a meager existence on government handouts and any other means necessary for survival. High unemployment forced many good people to enter the black market as a way of making money, and George was no different.

On day George brought Jacquie home to meet his family. Jacquie was stunned, as she had never seen poverty this close before. Her friend's negative views of communism were beginning to click; the inequities were horrifying and shattered Jacquie's sheltered view of life.

The seed was planted for a better life free from the grips and clutches of repressive communism. Jacquie's heart was broken as she faced the realization of leaving friends and family behind to find a better life in America. Maybe she would never see her family again. Jacquie,

George, and nine other brave freedom seekers were overwhelmed with excitement, fear, sadness, and joy. As Richie Havens proclaimed during Woodstock, "Freedom, freedom, freedom." Freedom was the internal tripwire that unleashed a torrent of resolve to find the resources and labor necessary to complete this incredible journey.

The difficult process of planning the 90-mile journey to freedom began to take a life of its own. They needed a boat, motor, food, and supplies to make the journey. Before long, the group's excitement was filled with frustration, disappointment, and the inevitable realization of the complexities of this dangerous oceanic voyage.

First, the group built the boat by finding an old bus, cutting it in half, and fitting it with an array of inflated inner tubes. Next, an old diesel engine would supply the necessary power for the boat by day, and a makeshift sail would power the boat by night. Ingeniously, the sail would also serve as a cover for protection from the tropical sun during the day. Lastly, a pig was slaughtered, and water was placed in containers, supplying the required nutrition and hydration for the four-day trip.

Using a compass, a primitive navigation map, and sheer determination, the group secretly left the island. The boat was launched for America, and the group was exhilarated. On a quest for freedom, the labor of their efforts had paid off, and they were on their way to freedom. Shortly after they took off, however, the group had to take an immediate detour. The Cuban authorities were searching for defectors, and the thought of being caught and thrown in jail was horrifying. The detour caused the boat to change course and to be entangled in treacherous mangroves. It took the group two days to leave the island and return to open water.

Again, the exhilaration was high and the taste of freedom was only 90 miles away. The group agreed to ration the food and water because of the unexpected detour, but spirits remained high. After four days, there was no land in sight. The group was experiencing bad weather, rip currents, and steamy tropical temperatures. To complicate matters, salt water contaminated their food. On day five, there was no food and very little fresh water.

Fear began to, surface and the group began to question the rationale of the trip. They argued, cried, and doubted their sanity for even undertaking this trip. They reminisced about family, friends, and the life they had left behind. There was clarity of their imminent danger and the stark reality of possible death. Still, the group forged on through day six and day seven even though tragedy threatened a member of the group. Uncle John, the group patriarch, was violently ill. In dire need of medical attention and water, Uncle John's health was rapidly deteriorating. Could their most anticipated fear become a reality?

After seven days at sea, the group continued to maintain composure, never losing sight of the treasured gift of freedom. As most slept, Jacquie was awakened by a calming presence. Her worst fears and emotions were soothed by a school of friendly dolphin. It was as if the dolphins were sent by a divine presence who heard the prayers and calls of the group. Day eight arrived with hope. The dolphins had navigated the boat through the night, then daybreak revealed the most incredible sight for eleven sick, weary, and hungry survivors—land!

As soon as the group saw the high-rise condominiums off the coast of Ft. Lauderdale, they began frantically rowing ashore. The sight of land and swaying palm trees was real. They were not dreaming or in the hereafter. They had made it! The group was met by caring Americans who provided food, medical attention, and shelter. The group ate, drank, and realized the heroic events of their eight-day trip. A picture of eleven courageous individuals next to a makeshift raft signifies the courage, caring, ingenuity, and motivation to live life to its fullest!

Humble Beginnings

Mary Rose grew up in very humble surroundings. She was the youngest of three siblings born to immigrant parents. Both parents had limited education and worked long hours in the family grocery store to make ends meet. When her parents arrived home after work, there was little energy or time left for personal nurturing and schoolwork. Her siblings were much older and left home, leaving Mary Rose to grow up as an only child. Throughout her childhood, she attended school and church events alone and learned life's harsh lessons quickly and painfully.

Early on, Mary Rose recognized an innate talent for academics and school. The gifted learner excelled, skipping second grade and graduating high school early. By the age of 18, she became a schoolteacher. The adversity of her lonely childhood became a catalyst for helping others. She remembered how the limitation of her father's literacy generated continual disappointment in her life. She stated how she just wanted a card that said, "Love Dad." Because of her father's limited education, however, cards for her only came signed with his surname. Mary Rose's disappointment and sadness fueled a passion for teaching.

Meanwhile, Mary Rose's close friend Sally developed a brain aneurism at the age of 47. Sally's world was immediately reduced to the simplest form of human existence, an existence requiring daily physical and emotional assistance to survive. The residual effect of the aneurism was also devastating for her family.

Sally lost her ability to recognize and communicate with family and friends. A heart-breaking moment came when Sally looked at a photograph of her children and asked, "Who are the children in the picture?"

The doctor's prognosis was that Sally would never have another original thought, but no one had more hope for Sally's recovery than Mary Rose. Mary Rose's innate motivation as a teacher and friend, fueled by an eternal compassion and faith, helped Sally look past the naysayers and begin the arduous road to recovery.

Upon reflection, Mary Rose identified how courage, fortitude, adaptability, perseverance, and prayer learned early in life became her internal support mechanism. Her innate positive compass became the beacon of light and acted as a roadmap for Sally's darkest days of rehabilitation. By selflessly giving herself to Sally's recovery, Mary Rose helped her friend connect the dots and connectors in her brain.

Slowly, Sally's brain began its miraculous process of healing and regeneration. The Sally everyone knew and loved began to emerge. Her wonderful smile, the mischievous glint in her eye, the familiar phrases everyone knew that she always said, demonstrated her rebirth, and it was the love of a friend, Mary Rose's, that motivated Sally through this rehabilitation and back to life. When most had given up, Mary Rose persevered and helped Sally succeed.

Twenty years later, Sally leads a normal life. She has driven her car throughout the country, knows the love of her children and grandchildren, and is a happy and productive woman in her community, thanks to Mary Rose's humble beginnings, which developed an inner strength to help and teach others to persevere through selfless love and irrevocable faith.

Realizing the Impossible Dream

Your inner motivation is the litmus test that determines personal success and failure. Do you give up easily or endure life's challenges? There are often things that seem too hard to accomplish; what makes you choose to accept or otherwise reject such challenges? When you are motivated to help others or to accomplish great things, you find an inner strength that keeps you on track even during the most difficult times.

Most people are considered "average Joes," and yet they face the daily trials and tribulations of life. Jacquie looked death in the eye with an inner knowing and fortitude not to give up. She made it to America. Many people have noble intentions and grandiose expectations and then fail. Motivation, combined with a strong positive inner attitude, can chart the road to success.

"Continual prodding of your motivation and measuring the results can secure your place at the table of success!"—Dr. Rich Contartesi

Dr. Rich's Prescription for Success

In order to maintain a successful level of motivation, you need to keep track of your progress. Measure and score where you are in relation to where you want to be. Each person discussed in this chapter set clear intentions and goals, and so should you. Doing so will allow you to reference your objectives and use them as your own measurement tool for achieving your goals.

1.   Where do you want to be one year from now?

_____
_____
_____
_____
_____

2.   What are the things that you need in order to achieve this? (Education, skills, financial resources, etc.)

_____
_____
_____
_____
_____

3.   Who can you count on to help you along the way? (Friends, parents, spouse, co-workers, etc.)

_____
_____

_____

_____

_____

4. How will you know that you have reached your
    goals?

_____

_____

_____

_____

5. How will you celebrate your success? (New clothes,
    car, vacation, etc.)

_____

_____

_____

_____

Chapter 9: The Motivating Quality in Leader Heroes

Dr. Rich Contartesi is currently the Chief Information and Accountability Officer for the School District of the City of Erie, Pennsylvania. He has over 27 years of urban K-12 experience and previously served as Associate Superintendent of Technology, Chief Technology Officer, Director of Instructional Technology, Director of Information Technology, and Business Systems Analyst. His experience provides a unique strategic and operational perspective to lead and integrate business operations, technology, and instruction.

Rich has developed and implemented enterprise financial systems, student information systems, data warehouse systems, and instructional learning systems. He holds a bachelor's degree in education, a Master of Business

Administration, and a Doctorate in Management and Organizational Leadership. Dr. Contartesi is an active participant in numerous technology and educational organizations.

CHAPTER 10

The Mentoring Quality in Leader Heroes

Contributed By Dr. Steven J. Minkin

"Mentoring is a brain to pick, an ear to listen, and a push in the right direction."— *John Crosby*

Mentor: to advise or train.

Titles such as life coaches, job mentors, senior executive mentors, trusted confidants, and personal accountability partners represent just a few ways you capture the role of mentor. The question is, how do you know when it is time to seek outside expertise and invest in a mentor? There is a formula to help determine when you need mentoring and how you should enter into that relationship.

For starters, both parties need to understand the framework for mentoring before establishing a relationship. Understanding the basic foundational elements in a mentoring relationship will help you make an informed decision on whether or not you are ready to pursue mentorship.

Taking time to explore each of the foundational mentoring elements and the types of mentoring relationships will allow you to determine what is best for you based on where you are, where you want to be, and what you want to achieve. Use the pre-mentor evaluation checklist to help you in this process. Once you determine that you can meet the foundational elements of a mentoring relationship, then you need to spend some time determining what type of mentor you need.

You build the foundation of any mentoring arrangement upon three key elements: relationship, communication, and timing. While all three are important, the element of relationship acts as the cornerstone for the foundation.

The First Element: Relationship

When you are in a mentoring relationship, there is a level of trust and deep relationship that needs to exist because of the nature of personal and professional information that is exchanged. With your mentor, remember that the deeper the relationship, the deeper the level of information that is exchanged, the more you will achieve. There are three characteristics to a solid relationship: trust, openness to feedback, and collaboration.

Trust: The Glue That Binds

Trust is the glue that holds any relationship together. Without it, a relationship will crumble and fall apart. The mentoring relationship is no different. It requires a strong element of trust between you and your mentor in order to succeed. The challenge becomes how to build trust. It takes time and requires mutual respect and professionalism. Respect, in turn, requires truthfulness, honesty, and integrity.

When you keep your word and follow through on what you say and exhibit consistent behavior, you are more likely to gain trust compared to those who do otherwise.

Trust can be equated to collateral in a bank account you hold with someone else. Every time you are truthful and honest, you invest in the bank account and increase your balance. When you are not truthful or honest, you withdraw from the account. It is that simple. Unlike most traditional banks that offer over-draft protection, there is no overdraft protection in the relationship bank. Withdraw more than you have invested, and you go broke. In many cases, a violation of trust can result in the end of the relationship.

The challenge with trust in mentoring is how you can build trust with someone you probably don't know that well. Often a mentoring relationship is the result of your being paired by an outside agency that manages linking people together. When you are matched with a stranger, you need to take some time to determine if you feel you can trust one another. In other situations, a mentor relationship may be formed with someone you have known for some time. A pre-established relationship holds a greater opportunity for success.

Receiving Feedback

The second element in a mentoring relationship is being open to feedback. A great mentoring relationship requires that you are able to speak about trouble spots, challenges, and obstacles. Often these reveal specific aspects of your personality that you may or may not recognize. A great mentor will discuss these areas with you to help you discover your opportunities for improvement.

If you enter a mentoring relationship and lack the humility to receive feedback, you are asking for disaster. You must not only understand this but also be willing to embrace it. Failing to do so is a waste of time for everyone involved. There is nothing worse than trying to help someone who is unwilling to grow. If you really want the true benefits of mentorship, you need to embrace feedback, apply it, and make the changes necessary for growth. This is how you unleash the power of mentoring.

Collaboration

We can find articles in a myriad of journals, papers, and books about the power of collaboration. Studies have shown that collaborative environments empower involved parties to develop more alternatives to situations and to create more effective courses of action. These improved courses of action allow leaders to make better decisions for their organizations, benefiting employees and customers.

Successful mentoring requires a collaborative approach as well. When the mentoring relationship operates at full effectiveness, both of you will grow from the relationship. You solicit feedback from your mentor, the mentor provides this feedback and recommendations to you, then you discuss them. You collaborate with your mentor to create a solid, focused action plan for you.

If these three elements can be created, or if they already exist between you and your mentor, then the foundation for the house of mentoring has been established.

The Second Element: Communication

The second foundational element of your mentor relationship is a communication plan. This plan must outline the type of communication medium(s) you will use with your mentor. This can be email, collaborative electronic white boards, telephone, face-to-face, or a creative combination depending on how you map what's best for the two of you. This sounds simple, yet it is an important component for both you and your mentor and should be discussed prior to starting your relationship.

The Third Element: Timing

You need to address the basic elements of timing with your mentor in order for the relationship to be most successful. The elements of timing include a commitment to invest time in the mentoring process, an agreement regarding the duration of the mentoring relationship, and a contract between you and your mentor that governs the process.

Mentoring takes time and is a key factor in a successful relationship. It is important to outline both parties' time commitment. Determine how much time each party is willing to commit to the mentor relationship. Some mentors arrange weekly meetings, while others are comfortable with monthly or even quarterly meetings. There is no textbook answer on how often a mentor should meet with you because each relationship is unique. The key is for you and your mentor to determine the frequency based on your needs, challenges, and circumstances, then create a schedule that works for both of you in achieving your needs and goals.

That's how you get started, but when and how do you stop? Mentoring relationships should have a discrete start and stop point. Failing to establish this time boundary can result in a relationship that drains the resources of time and energy from your mentor. Over time this can also lead to a situation where you no longer learn new skills, as you have outgrown your mentor.

At the beginning of the mentoring relationship, both of you need to come to an agreement regarding how long your mentor will serve in that role. This will likely take some deliberate thought and discovery to assess the level of effort required to assist you in achieving your goals.

The final step is to create a contract between you and your mentor. This step provides both of you an opportunity to spell out the rules for your relationship, including the communication plan, the level of involvement expected, and the length of time.

Also, it is important to include the purpose of the mentoring relationship and its desired outcomes. Having these elements captured in the contract allows both of you to stay focused on the purpose of the relationship and allows for termination of the relationship at any point if you have accomplished all of the objectives or have reached unmanageable or irresolvable issues in your relationship. There is no single standard for mentoring contracts, and a simple Internet search will turn up a myriad of templates from which to choose, modify, and adapt to fit your specific needs.

Creating a contract is the final step in developing a basis for a successful and beneficial mentoring relationship. It is important to invest some time up front in preparing and negotiating the contract so that you have a solid foundation, clean and clear communications, and upfront expectations outlined. This will ensure you are well on your way to a successful long-term relationship. With this foundation in place, the next step is to determine the type of mentor relationship that you are going to have.

Four Types of Mentoring Relationships

There are four main types of mentoring relationships: professional development, life skills development, leadership growth, or career advancement. Often mentoring discussions may cross over into one or more of these areas, but it is important to select the primary area where the majority of the mentoring will occur. This allows your mentor to bring a more specialized skill set, knowledge, and information to the table.

Professional Development

Mentoring for professional development relationships requires specific skills and knowledge from your mentor. Sharing these skills will make you more technically skilled at your job; this is the key point that separates this type of mentoring from that of career advancement. The focus of professional development mentoring is an increased level of technical skill. While this may result in career advancement, it is not the intended end state of this relationship type.

In the professional development relationship, the mentor will share job-specific wisdom and knowledge with you. This type of mentoring is similar to an internship, where the master artisan demonstrates the best way to accomplish a job. The tools used by the mentor in this type of relationship will include specific knowledge acquired through their years of experience, explicit knowledge, and extrapolating the meaning of both.

In terms of specific knowledge, the mentor should seek to share this information with you. Sharing this knowledge will allow you to acquire years of wisdom in a short period of time. Also, the mentor will teach you how to create understanding and meaning from information, which then empower you to become a visionary and a process improver. You can then harness the learning already accomplished by the organization and develop a new future by synthesizing explicit knowledge shared with you.

A professional development mentoring relationship requires some groundwork from both parties before you begin. Develop a list of topics you want to cover, then ask for specific areas in which your mentor feels he can assist you by providing specific knowledge.

Life Skills

Life skills mentoring relationships help you gain access to areas of knowledge and information that will increase your ability to be successful in several areas of life. Mentoring in the area of life development requires you to have an open mind to feedback regarding areas of improvement. There are two main pre-requisites for a successful life skills mentoring relationship. These include a willingness to accept feedback and the ability to look inward.

You must be willing to accept feedback and information that would require you to change. Personal change can be difficult and challenging. Your life skills mentor relationship, however, can provide a safe environment for you to learn, receive feedback, and change the areas of your life that need work.

The second element of a life skills development mentoring relationship is having the ability to look inward. Along with accepting feedback, you must also be able to evaluate your strengths and weaknesses. Doing so will allow you to receive new information, internalize it, and apply it to the way you think about and view the world. Self-reflection allows you to solve areas of personal weakness with the help of a mentor to adjust your life and worldview.

In addition to improving both personal and professional skills, this type of mentoring educates you on how to receive constructive feedback. More importantly, this type of relationship teaches you to take the feedback, take action, and facilitate a life change.

Leadership Development

Mentoring relationships can help groom or develop your leadership skills. This type of relationship not only helps you grow as a leader but also molds the next generation of leaders in an organization. A leadership development mentoring relationship should focus on four foundational leadership areas: vision casting, goal setting, time management, and communication skills.

Vision casting and goal setting are two skills any developing leader must come to understand. Organizations with a strategic vision are better at linking activities to a specific strategy. Linking activities to a strategy allows organizational leadership to determine courses of action to pursue based on the strategy. To develop a strategy, leaders need to be able to create a vision for the future as it relates to their organization.

A mentor that can guide you through the process of exploring the world, understanding how it is changing, and defining a future state is a valuable mentor to have. Once you have the ability to create a vision of the future, the next step is to create goals that link the vision to actionable steps that move the organization, department, or team towards achieving that vision. Working with a trusted mentor can develop your ability to see the future and make it happen.

The demands on a leader are many regardless of the level they work at in an organization. Time management is another area in which your mentor should work with you. Understanding how to manage personal and professional time to achieve desired outcomes is an important addition to a leader's toolbox.

While there are many commercially available systems to assist with time management, a mentor should guide you through an evaluation of these systems to find the one that is best suited for you. Time management is more than just getting a lot done in a predetermined period of time. It is about maintaining a balance between personal and professional development, self-empowerment, and personal growth to effect change in a larger circle of influence.

Effective communication is a key element of any leadership development plan. In today's world of virtual and face-to-face communication, leaders need to be skilled at sharing their thoughts, vision, ideas, and dreams across a wide variety of platforms. A mentor will help you understand the challenges of virtual communication and leadership as well as provide insights on how to communicate effectively in a traditional setting.

While leadership development mentoring can cover a wide range of topics, these four areas are foundational leadership skills. Once your mentor is confident that you have a strong understanding and mastery of these skills, the doors are open for a whole host of other leadership topics. These may include delegation, transformational leadership, leading change, understanding organizational culture, and influencing up. This is not designed to be a comprehensive list, merely a starting point for you.

Career Advancement

The final type of mentoring relationship is aimed at helping you advance your career. This relationship provides you with face time with leaders within the organization. While the topics of personal growth, life skills, and leadership development will undoubtedly appear during the relationship, the focus of your attention is seeking face time with senior leaders.

While there may be some mentoring that does occur in the career advancement relationship, you must be clear about your purpose before starting such a mentoring relationship. Failing to desire self-improvement or development will become clear to your mentor at some point in the relationship. Selfish ambition may also cause the relationship to backfire and lead to the termination of your mentoring relationship.

If used correctly, a career advancement mentoring relationship will allow you to have a senior leader who provides you with a future road map for career development. Learning what jobs to take in pursuit of advancement in the organization can be a wonderful outcome of this type of relationship. Another benefit of career advancement mentoring is exposure to high-level strategic issues in an organization.

Career advancement mentoring relationships have the potential for great learning and development. Take note, however, that entering to these relationships with the wrong intention can create a less than positive outcome.

"People often teach best what they most desire to learn." Anonymous

Dr. Rich's Prescription for Success

Mentoring is a process where you can grow and benefit from years of experience and learn from a seasoned mentor. Before entering such a relationship, however, evaluate the foundational elements required in a successful mentoring relationship. Both you and your mentor must trust each other, determine and agree on a time commitment, and identify the frequency of meetings before determining the length of time for the relationship.

Once your mentoring contract captures your foundational elements, you and your mentor need to agree on the type of mentoring that you desire. This could be professional development, where you seek to increase your technical skills and abilities; life skills development, where you want to improve your abilities personally and professionally; leadership growth, which helps you develop across a wide range of leadership skills; or career advancement, which exposes you to strategic issues and leadership within an organization.

Regardless of the type of mentoring relationship you enter, the potential for learning and development is tremendous. Not only will you leave the relationship with new tools and skills, but usually your mentor grows with you as well. When you have an effective relationship, your mentor is as much a student as you are.

Chapter 10: The Mentoring Quality in Leader Heroes

Dr. Steven J. Minkin has over 19 years of experience as an active duty military officer. He earned his Doctor of Management in Organizational Leadership Degree from the University of Phoenix. He has been published in *The International Journal of Networking and Virtual Organizations*, the *Air Power Journal*, including the English, French, and Portuguese editions. His articles have appeared in the *Armed Forces Comptroller Magazine*, the *Air Force Comptroller Magazine*, and Air University's *Wright Flyer*. He was recognized as the Assistant Secretary of the Air Force for Financial Management's Author of the Year in 2006. Dr. Minkin can be contacted at MgtDrSteve@yahoo.com

Chapter 11

The Teacher Quality
in Leader Heroes

"The teacher who is indeed wise does not bid you to enter the house of his wisdom but rather leads you to the threshold of your mind."—Khalil Gibran

Teacher: one whose occupation is to instruct. But many teachers teach not as a job but only to help others learn.

Leader heroes are teachers. These heroes may not teach formal school lessons; they may just have set a shining example for others to follow and emulate. Teaching heroes leave lifelong impressions. Teaching comes in many forms, through different vehicles, and with different results. The old saying "when the student is ready, the teacher will appear" is more real than most believe.

There are, of course, teachers who have a career in formal education, but there are others who teach with no formal education and are still teachers in every sense of the word. Everyday teacher heroes are those who take their knowledge and share it with others. Some of these teacher heroes do not even know they are teaching; they are just being themselves and offering assistance or advice.

Career teachers are found in every academic institution, whether it be in preschool, kindergarten, grade and high school, trade schools or in higher education. Teachers are also found outside academic institutions. They can be found in sports organizations, scouting troops, or fraternal organizations; it can be a neighbor down the street, a colleague in the workplace, or a fellow devotee in your place of worship. Wherever you find people who care about one another and want to make the world a better place, you will find teacher heroes.

A teacher hero is willing to take what they know and share it with others. Some do it for money, but most everyday teacher heroes do not care about being paid. Even family members such as parents, grandparents, uncles, aunts, siblings and others can be teacher heroes. Teacher heroes are those whom we remember the most because they shared their lessons with us when we were at a troublesome or exciting time in our lives.

Formal and Informal Teacher Heroes

I have a number of formal and informal teachers who have made a long-lasting impression on me. Whether

I was in grade school or high school ready to learn a lesson such as mathematics, or in the United States Navy when I had to learn how to become a sailor, I have fond memories of many teacher heroes. Even now, with a doctoral degree and all my successes, teachers come and go when I need them the most to teach me a lesson I have yet to learn or need to learn again.

I lost my father at a young age, so some of the early teacher heroes in my life were fathers of my friends. These men realized that my widowed mother had her hands full with two young children. These men

often came to my mother's rescue by helping me learn how to change a tire on a bicycle (Mr. Heise, we never called him by his first name) or sitting me down for a stern talking-to (Sam Vitalo, we could him by his first name) and playing the role of father figure when I needed direction or correction.

Who in your early life left a lasting impression upon you as a teacher hero?

Name: _____

Role in your Life: _____

City/State/Country: _____

Other teacher heroes in my life were from grade school and high school. They taught lessons in unique ways. While it was their paid jobs, these teacher heroes went beyond their job descriptions to provide not just a formal education but also life development. In high school, some of the best teachers are those who relate to and communicate with teenage students the best. They do not see themselves as authoritative figures required to stand in front of the classroom and lecture kids. Rather, they find ways to reach teenagers with care, fun, and knowledge. These memorable teacher heroes are those who are able to break through, educate, and inspire.

Life-Changing Teacher Hero

In high school, my favorite teacher was Mr. John Watts. He taught me a life lesson about myself more valuable than any formal classroom lesson he was paid to teach. Mr. Watts was there for me at a time when I was doubting my decision in 1975 to join the United States Navy.

In my junior year of high school, I decided that upon graduation I was going to enlist in the service. I found great value in the groups I belonged to as a boy— groups such as the Boy Scouts, Sea Explorers (a division of the Boy Scouts), and high school ROTC. I thrived in the structure of these types of groups then and, to this day, continue to enjoy such a structured environment.

In February of my senior year of high school, I enlisted in the Navy's delayed entry program that allowed me to go on active duty in August after graduation. As I started to tell my friends that I had joined the Navy, many tried to talk me out of it. Not only did they wonder why I would do such a thing, but they chastised me for it as well. In part, this was understandable since for some of them, their older brothers were coming back from the Vietnam War and had some vivid experiences. And, unfortunately for a few of them, their brothers lost their life in the war. Moreover, this was a time when the Vietnam War was coming to a close, and the sentiments about joining the military in the United States were neither high nor positive.

Mr. Watts saw my inner conflict and the peer pressure I was experiencing. When he noticed I was starting to question my choice, he pulled me aside and taught me a lesson I will never forget. It had nothing to do with his class and nothing to do with the high school curriculum or any part of his job description. What Mr. Watts told me is that once I have identified what I am passionate about and what I want to do, I should never let anybody who knows less than me talk me down or make me change my mind, even if those naysayers are my best friends or people that I trust.

I went into the Navy with the intention of staying enlisted for 4 years; I stayed 23 years before I retired. To this day, I believe it is the best life decision I have ever made. The Navy took me to new places and to different countries where I met new people. More importantly, it allowed me to grow up and mature, both physically and mentally. The Navy made a man out of the boy that I was and gave me a life and career beyond what was too often a sad alternative in my hometown, the South Side of Chicago.

My High School Teacher Hero

Mr. John Watts, High School Teacher, Chicago, Illinois

Mr. Watts changed my life with his advice and sound counsel to follow my dreams and life passions.

Dr. Rich Schuttler

My passion and my dreams were different and far beyond those of my friends—not better, just different. I followed my dreams. Since then, I have always lived and continue to live my life on my own terms. Mr. Watts set the pace for me when I was 17 years old. Without him, I'm not sure if I would have followed through with my choice.

Everyone I've talked with has a *Mr. Watts* example, a teacher hero that they remember. While the reasons vary, these inspiring teachers provided a lifelong lesson that remains unforgotten. Teacher heroes like Mr. Watts change lives, yet it is often the case that they don't realize the impact they have on the lives of others. It is with great regret that I never reached out to thank him for his insights. Years went by, and when I finally thought to reach out, he had already passed away years prior. I hope that he knows how valuable he was to me and to many others.

The Student Becomes a Teacher

Some of my teacher heroes, like Mr. Watts, set an example for me. Perhaps that's why I became a teacher—a university faculty member. I decided to become a teacher not by plan but more so because I fell into it. It feels like teaching is my destiny because of all the work I have done and continue to do. Nothing brings me more pleasure than teaching.

The Navy trained me as an electronics technician. That training allowed me to build a significant level of subject matter expertise. After seven years of experience, I was given the opportunity to teach at one of the duty stations.

I taught for the first time, and I thoroughly enjoyed it! Then, I started to go to college at night to work on my bachelor's degree, so I taught during the day and studied at night. What's interesting is that I had never really liked school before that, but at that point in the Navy I had reached a level of maturity wherein I realized that schooling was essential for advancement.

After three years of teaching for the Navy, I realized how it was a deep-rooted passion of mine. What I really enjoyed was taking a student who knew very little about complex electronic circuits and then guiding them to see something they could not see and do before. My love of teaching showed. I was awarded the Navy's Master Trainer Specialist designation.

Education has a way of creating new views and a way of providing motivation and self-accomplishment. As a teacher, I was able to see in other people's eyes their hopes and aspirations, the same sort of hopes and aspirations I had felt when I went to class. A teacher hero can leave a lifelong impression, and I gain satisfaction from doing the same. Perhaps this is why I started my online membership site Professional Progress Academy to help educate and train others around the world.

Tangible and Intangibles

Education is both tangible and intangible. Once educated, no one can ever take your knowledge away. Unfortunately, I found it is also something too many people paid for, received, and yet neglect to use. Not everyone who graduates with a degree gains the insightful wisdom that can come from the educational process. For the wrong reasons, some focus more on earning a certain grade point average and completing their program as quickly as they can to graduate, only to realize years later that they had in fact failed to learn the essence of the coursework.

I have seen this for many years in many different people in every industry. There are those who have bachelor's, master's, and even doctoral degrees and yet are unable to self-assess or self-reflect on the lessons of the curriculum. I always suspected that this type of thing was not out of the ordinary, as occasionally I would see senior leaders in organizations who seemed rather incompetent. I found this out firsthand when I was a Dean in the School of Advanced Studies at the University of Phoenix and I was responsible for hiring faculty. About 25 percent of the candidates who applied for open teaching positions were not well-versed in their content areas, yet 100 percent had the requisite degrees to qualify them for the position. Too many had the degree but not the education. Too many were "certified but not qualified."

A teacher hero is one who facilitates curriculum and ensures that his students learn not only the basic information but also how and when to apply that information. There is no way to ensure students gain the insights for practical application of class material, but a good teacher hero will spend time and effort helping to reduce the amount of graduates who earn the degree but fail to learn the education. Some of the best teacher heroes are those who can reduce complex theories to practical application steps and help others to do the same.

Teacher heroes come in one's life at different times. I had teachers to help me learn the knowledge and to build self-confidence. Of course I learned the content as well; I passed tests and shared conversations that reflected my comprehension of the material. Then a different teacher in the workplace taught me how to master my career field. This teacher had been doing the work for a number of years and was an expert. This person had already transitioned from learned knowledge to becoming an expert. This was the same field in which I wanted to become an expert.

Learning Cycle

Those involved in formalized education will more easily see learning cycles. Others more than likely know of the concept but may not be familiar with the formalities or theoretical perspective of the learning cycle. The learning cycle tends to be intuitive. All teacher heroes lived their own learning cycles and later shared the results of those learning cycles with others.

After a number of years of experience and of my possession of a formalized academic education, I noticed a learning cycle I was moving through based on my gained knowledge and hands-on experience. Experience is a great educator. It is much like the learning that comes from touching a hot stove that burns the skin. Some lessons we hope to not repeat, yet others we are destined to relearn several times throughout our life.

At a young age, I became was able to take different experiences and uncover patterns. More so, I started to see how parts formed a system or an organization. I was able to analyze and separate; connect one step to the next; to classify, arrange, compare and explain. These cycles of learning over time made me a subject matter expert much like many others I admire. By observing the teacher heroes in my life, I was able to refine my own learning styles and cycles.

Figure 1 is an adaptation of Benjamin Bloom's cognitive taxonomy. While I was living the steps in the below model, it was not until years later when I was an Associate Dean at the University of Phoenix when I learned there was an actual model to reflect what I had lived years prior.

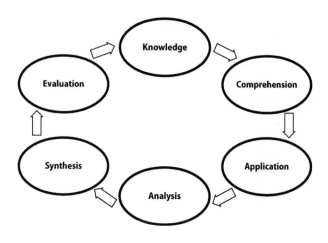

Figure 10.1—Learning cycles according to Benjamin Bloom's Cognitive Taxonomy

As my experience accumulated during learning cycles, I matured enough to be able to synthesize different views and experiences to solve complex problems and improve processes. The learning cycles, when a teacher hero was not around, helped me to gain new ideas beyond what was in front of me. I started to predict and draw conclusions about what was happening and how I could make things better. The same experience I reflect upon happens to many and in most instances everyday leader heroes have gone through a similar experience.

From a synthesis of many experiences, the next step was the evaluation stage. I was able to compare and discriminate between ideas. I became capable of verifying the value of evidence. I was able to assess and decide. I was even able to make valid conclusions and comparisons. I was able to summarize for others what I was discussing in a way that they could understand, just like the teacher heroes who taught me.

Oftentimes the evaluation results gave me new data or insights that would send me back into the learning cycle to the beginning stage of knowledge. This was because evaluation produced new knowledge. As the cycle repeated, I had to again comprehend that knowledge, analyze and synthesize. The learning cycle is the essence of what many refer to as being a lifelong learner.

The cycle of learning is what one must do to become a master, to be an expert, to become someone worthy of teaching others. Concrete experiences over a number of years allow one to be able to observe and reflect upon what they have experienced. From observations and reflections, one is able to conceptualize opportunities for improvement. From conceptualization, one is able to experiment with what they believe or to consider the premise to find out whether something is true or not.

It takes years to become an expert, yet today too many want to go from book knowledge to being an expert and then wonder why they aren't more successful than they expected to be. Then there are those who want to go from only practical, hands-on experience and want to be an expert even without at least some formal education. However, in an ideal world there must be a balance in education and expertise to become an expert qualified to teach and worthy of emulation.

A Final Thought

A teacher hero leaves a fingerprint in another's mind. They leave a lasting impression that never goes away. Each teacher hero is unique in their own ways, but they are all masters of knowledge at what they do and are worthy of emulation. Teacher heroes make the world a better place and offer lifelong learning opportunities to move from a classroom or one-on-one setting to becoming a student of life.

"Education is a lot like life itself; the more you put into it, the more you'll get out of it."

- Dr. Rich Schuttler

Dr. Rich's Prescription for Success

Who are the three teacher heroes who left their lasting fingerprint on your mind and what do you remember most about them?

_____

_____

_____

Pay it Forward

Consider finding email addresses or a mailing address and send each of your teacher heroes a thank-you note acknowledging their contribution in your life. Send something tangible that they can later share with others or put into their scrapbook that family generations can read. Such an act of goodwill on your part will help your leader heroes realize the impact they have made in your life. Unless you do something like this, they may never know how important they were to you.

If one or more of your teacher heroes has passed away, consider sending the thank-you note to their relative so that they can know how much you appreciate their loved one. If it was a grade school or high school teacher and you cannot find him, send your thank-you note to the current school principal. Giving away such praise can make the recipient's day and will help you to be more open to saying thank you to those who have helped and will continue to help you in such important and memorable ways. A kind gesture does indeed hold such power!

Chapter 11: The Teacher Quality in Leader Heroes

Dr. Rich Schuttler

CHAPTER 12

The Positive Quality Leader Heroes

Contributed by Helene Summer Medena

"A person who has good thoughts cannot ever be ugly. You can have a wonky nose and a crooked mouth and a double chin and stick-out teeth, but if you have good thoughts, they will shine out of your face like sunbeams and you will always look lovely."—Roald Dahl

Positive: consisting in or characterized by the presence or possession of features or qualities rather than their absence.

Leading with Force

People who lead with force are often filled with negativity and use threats and punishment. They make false promises, use intimidation, attempt to terrorize, pressure and are often dictators whose primary means of leading is fear. Examples of such leaders are Adolph Hitler, Idi Amin, Stalin, and Osama Bin Laden.

Leading with Inspiration

People who lead with inspiration are filled with positivity. They provide encouragement and genuine support. They are filled with vitality, and they exhibit true caring, consideration, compassion, enthusiasm and stimulation. Examples of these kinds of leaders are Martin Luther King, Gandhi, Abraham Lincoln, Helen Keller and Mother Theresa. These inspirational leaders give followers hope, warmth and satisfaction with their work and themselves.

Adolph Hitler and Mahatma Gandhi were both very powerful leaders from different times in history. Both had devoted followers and both made a significant difference on the planet. In spite of the differences each made, there seems to be something inherently wrong with even having the two names in the same sentence. One caused horrific acts of violence, while the other sacrificed his life helping others.

Hitler led with force for a single weak followership, whereas Gandhi led with inspiration for the masses. Gandhi's vision was larger than any issue at hand and larger than a single nation. His philosophy is known worldwide and continues to be used to resolve conflicts in organizations and individual homes. Leaders who apply Gandhi's philosophy can touch everyone with whom they come into contact; they can help them become true positive leader heroes.

Positive leaders are generous with praise. They are supportive to those around them and are willing to be involved in a positive manner when both personal and professional problems exist. These kinds of leaders live in a positive world and have a positive outlook. Their enthusiasm and energy is contagious and desirable. They inject "something good" into every project and are grateful for and willing to share all their accomplishments. When positive leaders show up, followers feel their vitality, energy, and uplifting outlook on life. Positive leaders are perceived as vibrant, energetic people regardless of their age.

Cynics sometimes criticize their energy, but that doesn't pull positive leader heroes down. Because they are transformational leaders, they inspire people to follow them willingly and to work beyond expectations. Their positive manner demonstrates to followers how to keep a sense of humor, which helps to take some of the stress out of work and life, thus adding fun to much of what the followers are asked to do.

The Myth of Pollyanna

Pollyanna is a bestselling novel written by Eleanor Porter in 1913. The main character is a young orphan girl, Pollyanna, who ends up living with her wealthy but harsh aunt. Pollyanna's life centers on what she called the Glad Game, a positive attitude she learned from her dad. The essence of the game is to find something to be glad about in every situation. The game started on Christmas when Pollyanna was hoping for a doll. What she found was a pair of crutches. Making the game up on the spot Pollyanna's father taught her to look at the positive side of the situation. In this case he wanted Pollyanna to be glad about the crutches because "she didn't need them."

With this philosophy, her own sunny personality and sincere, sympathetic soul, Pollyanna brought great gladness to her dispirited New England town that she transformed into a pleasant place to live. The Glad Game shielded her from her aunt's demanding attitude. Just with her presence, Pollyanna was teaching the citizens of her town to play the game as well. She transformed the citizenry without even knowing it.

The Pollyanna attitude is one of hope and happiness that is in search of all things positive. The best way to make people love you is to bring lovely energy and kindness when you show up. That is the real Pollyanna attitude. It is the mindset that will help people grow.

Positive leaders are much like Pollyanna. They stand out because they are rare and they have the same characteristics as Pollyanna. They work hard to find the good in their organizations and their followers. They don't focus on the negative. The downside of being this kind of leader is that those who are not positive leaders often criticize others for being "too positive." People sometimes roll their eyes and make comments such as, "Oh, she is such a Pollyanna." It demonstrates how easy it is for people to be negative and criticize those who aren't. It is particularly annoying to hear that kind of comment from people whom you know don't even know the story about Pollyanna. With this kind of negative commentary from negative people, when you hear someone call you a Pollyanna, consider it a compliment.

> *"Let us rise and be thankful, for if we didn't learn a lot today, at least we learned a little, and if we didn't learn a little, at least we didn't get sick, and if we got sick, at least we didn't die; so let us all be thankful."*—Buddha

From Negative to Positive

Every child deserves to be happy and have a beautiful, safe childhood. However, in this particular time in our history, it is getting more difficult for children to have a beautiful and safe childhood. As hard as parents try to be protective, loving and supportive, there are times when children get ill, have their knee scratched, or as they get older, find their hearts broken. But just like Pollyanna, if we can get children to think positively during difficult and painful times, they will develop a strong and positive character as they go through life. When children experience the common negative or painful experiences described above, parent leaders need to help them understand that the pain and suffering they experience is the same as what others are experiencing, or that it can even be a lot worse for millions of others. Life is only as bad as we allow it to be.

> *"There is a little difference in people, but that little difference makes a big difference. The little difference is attitude. The big difference is whether it is positive or negative."*—W. Clement Stone

"I was a happy little girl growing up in a dysfunctional family but I didn't know life could be any different. Life at home for me seemed normal. In the fifth grade, bullies started daily attacks and it didn't take too long before the happy little girl disappeared. My thoughts became dark. I was shy and withdrawn. I was always lonely, scared and bitter about life. I had no self-esteem. I became negative. When my body started changing from a little girl to a young lady, I experienced a complete new set of self-criticisms. I didn't like myself. I didn't like my life. I didn't like anything about my existence.

In 1991, the Croatian Independence War began. My twin sister and I were separated. My brother was a soldier stationed on the front line. My grandmother's house was bombed. My best friend died. I was given 20 minutes to pack all of my belongings into one plastic bag and leave what was left of what I knew as a home and my life. I became a refugee in my own country. By the age of 16, I had seen things no child should ever see. I lost hope in life and humanity. Nothing made sense. I could see nothing positive about the future. Why bother trying to be positive? What was the purpose? It seemed as if there would be no end to suffering. I believed I had nothing to hope for anymore.

Everything I experienced up to that point was too horrible to describe or to even want to remember but I was still alive. Most people my age would have had good reason to be suicidal. So why did I still wake up in the morning and want a warm blanket, to hear laughter, to play music? That was a fascinating phenomenon to me. What I soon realized is that it was the positive side of me still trying to come out. It meant I actually wanted to live a positive, not a bitter life. I didn't know what that kind of life might actually look like, but I knew I wanted it. I wanted it so much that it became the driving force of my daily being.

Eventually I ran away from the refugee camp, and in my quest to taste and create a positive life I traveled the world, read hundreds of books, changed my diet, my living conditions and ultimately became a nun. People who knew me before my change to a positive life would see me and ask, 'Really? You? You are a nun? My answer was, 'Yes, it's me—a nun.'

The point in sharing my journey has nothing to do with religion. It has everything to do with the desire to find that once happy little girl in myself again. The point is to share with you to never let go of the desire to eliminate the negative and find your positive self. I consider what I experience as the price one pays to change life and became a positive person. Because I was looking to create a happy life for myself I created the motto, 'Life is short. Live Delicious.' That motto became my passion, my purpose, my lifestyle and nobody knew about it.

One day a friend I hadn't seen in a long time said 'Helena, there is something different about you.' I replied, 'No there isn't.' She said 'Yes, there is.' I thought nothing of it. Then, another person said something similar, and yet another person. Then I noticed people enjoyed being around me. I was becoming a positive person.

Recently, my friend went to a spa and talked about me with the staff. The hair stylist said, 'Yes, I know Helena. She is always so positive. She is the happiest person I know.' If she only knew how negative and bitter I was before."

- Helena Summer Medena

How to Develop Positivity

"Watch your thoughts before they become your words. Watch your words before they become your actions. Watch your actions before they become your habits. Watch your habits before they become your character. Watch your character before it becomes your destiny."—Unknown

The formula to use involves three steps plus one secret ingredient:

1. **Stop**. Stop doing what doesn't work for you. Stop hiding your power. Stop playing small. Stop criticizing others. Stop criticizing yourself. Stop whining, complaining, restraining, and weight gaining. You know what doesn't work for you, so stop!

2. **Take a Breath**. Relax, slow down, rest and let go. Think a little, feel a little, without any strain or force.

Be present right here, right now. Take a breather, don't rush, chill out, smell the roses, or plant the roses. You know what brings you peace, what gets you centered. Do those things.

3. **Take a Step**. Take a step towards wherever it is you want to go. Follow your inner "yes" guide. Do you know what is driving your aliveness? If you have difficulties finding out what feels like a "yes" to you, think about three things you can do today that will make your life more pleasant, more beautiful and sweeter. It might be going for a walk or swim, calling your parents or friends, eating a few fresh strawberries, singing, dancing, or meditating.

If you follow the three steps above, there is no guarantee you will automatically have a positive life. Why? There is one hidden secret ingredient that must also be present—**fun**.

Yes, fun! When baking bread, salt is actually less than one percent of all the ingredients, but it is one hundred percent of the flavor. Your work, your family, your dreams and goals would have no flavor if there is no fun associated with them. I'm not talking about crazy sex, drugs, alcohol or other bizarre kinds of fun. I am talking about lively, warm, pleasing and perhaps, a little cheeky fun.

The three steps and the secret ingredient will open your mind. An open mind is a free mind. A free mind thinks, plays and stays positive. An open mind will bring you into your reality and the reality that other positive people have. Slowly but surely, one day a friend will come to you and say, "You know, there is something different about you." You will disagree, but they will insist that there is something different. You can then just smile knowing you are now a more positive person, a positive leader hero.

Words, Words, Words–the Key to Positivity

There is only one part of the entire universe you can be certain that you have control over, and that is your words. The paradox is that most people don't want to believe it. "Oh no, it can't be that simple," is what most people believe. In fact, it is that simple and it is more powerful than we can grasp. Think about it. Positive people use positive words. Negative people use negative words. We can only pretend until we start talking. Eventually the truth reveals itself.

> *"You have it easy in your power to increase the sum total of this world's happiness now. How? By giving a few words of sincere appreciation to someone who is lonely or discouraged. Perhaps you will forget tomorrow the kind words you say today, but the recipient may cherish them over a lifetime."*—Dale Carnegie

Here is an experiment that may convince you about the power of words. Read the sentences below aloud three times, text it to three of your friends, put it as your Facebook status and call your mother and read it to her.

> "Life is very beautiful. I'm reading a great book. My mind is clear and full of ideas. I am getting stronger every day and my vision is sharp. I love it!"

How do you feel doing this? It should feel uplifting and joyful; it should give you a sense of certainty and appreciation. How do you think your friends will respond? Do you think your mom will be glad to hear it?

Now, do the same with the sentence below.

> "Life really sucks. I'm stuck watching TV and my mind is delusional and paranoid. I am rapidly developing cancer and I am going blind. I hate it!"

How do you feel now? If you haven't read the sentence three times, it means you already believe in the power of words. If you read it, how does it feel? Not very good, right? Are you convinced yet? Positive people speak positive words. Fill your mind with positive words by reading books such as this one and other kinds of books such as biographies or fiction.

"I don't think of all the misery, but of the beauty that still remains."—Anne Frank

Where to Find Positivity–Infected Leaders

"Argue for your limitations, and sure enough, they are yours."—Richard Bach

Books open your mind. There are many positive authors who will enrich your life and help you develop positive qualities—all of it, just by reading books. Richard Bach is a well-respected author whose works many people enjoy.

Besides being an author, he is also a pilot and owns a bi-plane. He loves barnstorming or flying the plane around farms and places where planes don't usually go. The plane can land almost anywhere, so Richard would often take his plane, fly low over the farms and when people would wave at him, he would circle around, land the plane and chat with them. Soon children would come running, their eyes wide as baseballs, looking at the huge propeller on the Searman, its double wings swaying up and down with the gentle wind. Richard would ask if anyone wanted to ride.

The children would squeal with delight, their hands raised high in the sky as they shouted, "Yes!" Richard would choose the first one, usually the shyest or quietest one, and strap them onto the front seat of the plane. With the sound of thunder, the great flying machine would roar to life, smoke billowing from the sides as the 800-horsepower engine came alive. Richard would click his microphone and ask his little co-pilot if he or she was ready. Two little thumbs reach for the sky to indicate readiness and the plane would lift off the ground and fly into the blue sky. After a 15-minute thrill, Richard would land back onto the ground, lift his co-pilot out and the child would stand in front of his friends shy no more. He would scream from the top of his lungs, "That was the best ride of my life!"

For the rest of the afternoon, 15 minutes at a time, Richard would give a few farm children the ride of their lives, something none of them would ever forget. He led them to the sky. He led them to freedom from their limitations and doubts. He showed them what they could do. His actions showed he was a leader. His books show he had big visions of life and when you read them, his words can do to your heart what the plane rides did for the children.

"Bad things are not the worst things that can happen to us. Nothing is the worst thing that can happen to us!"
—Richard Bach

Positive Challenge

Take up the challenge of increasing your positivity for 30 days. "Positivize" your thoughts, words and actions. Invite friends to join you, or just keep it to yourself and make the world a better place with your presence. When you think something negative, turn it around. Remember the affirmation, "Only good will come from it," then think of three positive things that can come out of it.

When you say something negative, stop and say, "What I meant to say was…" then replace it with a positive, uplifting statement that encourages you and that has a spark of life in it.

When you do something you regret, go ahead and apologize and do something beautiful and positive to three other people. Pay it forward! Play Pollyanna's Glad Game. Watch biographies of positive leaders, read positive quotes, read positive books and always answer the phone with a smile in your voice and on your face. Even though the caller cannot see you, he will notice that smile.

"There are only two ways of moving from one point to another. One is away from the negativity you don't want. The other is towards the positivity we do want."—Helena Summer Medena

Dr. Rich's Prescription for Success

Go show up and make the world a better place. Show up with your kindness, not with your story. Show up with your love, not your resentment. Show up with your open heart. Bring sunshine with you and if you see someone without a smile on his face, give him one.

Stand out by liking people, and you will find they are as likeable as you are. When you do it, the worst-case scenario is that you will be happier and more fun for others to be around you. The best-case scenario is that you will be happier, more fun to be with, and your goals will be fulfilled. Life is for the living. Make it a positive, life-long lasting delicious experience!

Chapter 12: The Positive Quality in Leader Heroes

Helena Summer Medena was born in Croatia. The war shattered her teenage dreams and took the life of her best friend. From shelters to refugee camps, Helena learned survival skills and grew up quickly. She wanted to remove bitterness out of life and, therefore, passionately studied spirituality, healing arts, mind power, meditation, yoga, NLP, and EFT. These tools work. Passion works. Purpose works.

Now Helena lives in Hawaii and is excited about seeing "from bitter to delicious" makeovers. She gracefully helps people lighten up. They find joy and passion, make more money, and develop relationships that shine. According to Helena, "*With the desire to create a happy life for myself, I named my brand LIV DELICIOUS. We teach what we most need to learn.*" For more about Helena, visit www.LivDelicious.com